Praise for David Mehler's
Bad is Bent Good
* * *

"So 'Dave Mehler drives a truck at a landfill in Portland, Oregon, and the poems in *Bad Is Bent Good* detail that place and its people.' That's a true statement, yet a statement so inadequate that it should probably qualify as a lie. With a preternatural attention to detail and dense, fastidious articulation, Mehler draws his world—and he draws us into it. Once we're there, and once we learn to breathe the fetid atmosphere of his claustrophobic version of Gehenna, a miracle happens: we discover that his smoldering paracosm is filled with iterations of the familiar. Here they are, the very things that make our own everyday versions of the world: kindness, stupidity, empathy, vanity, brilliancy, and all the rest. And even while the worst of what we've thrown to the curb (human and inhuman) is being scrambled, broken, and buried in its final resting place—persistently, resiliently, triumphantly, nature breaks through in all its broken beauty. I can think of no work—even of fantasy or science fiction—that has pulled me so thoroughly into a place further from my own, or into a more fully realized not-quite-alternate reality. *Bad Is Bent Good* may be one of the strangest books I've ever read—and one of the most deeply human."

— Bill Jolliff, author of *At Rest in My Father's House* and *Twisted Shapes of Light*

"The dump is where the human story goes to lie in its fragments. What could be more American than tending this particular kind of melting pot? Importantly, these poems search for meaning, but not merely through subject or social concern; rather, form and a matter-of-fact narrative gusto insist on our rapt attention. The directness, the unapologetic honoring of lives squirrelled away at the margins, and the way these poems ultimately search for human tenderness among the ruins make *Bad Is Bent Good* worthy of our highest praise. An unwavering book."

— Michael McGriff, author of *Eternal Sentences* and *Home Burial*

"As if everything not underwater is on fire..."

—Mal Westcott

"I can think of no better Virgil-like guide than Dave Mehler to tour a reader through the inferno of a modern landfill; a stratified depository of smashed things and smashed lives. But though broken, not all lives are smashed. Mehler's reporting is unsparing, yet humane. Every soul he speaks of is just that—a soul, not a mere abstraction. No matter how trapped, fractured, or just plain bored, these people are real, their unique array of hopes, fears, griefs, and small satisfactions finding their echo in the mind and heart of any attentive, empathic reader."

—Keith Hansen, Drywall Contractor

"The writing in this collection is not only born of the labor, the love, the real people of the American Experiment, but of a genre-defying poetic reality that we can see, taste, smell, and feel, *profoundly*. The places these hefty, roiling, Whitmanesque poems of the land

and of the open road will take you to are the normally off-limits, prohibited realms no one ever gets to know . . . from which you will never ever be able to return."

—Philip Kobylarz, author of *A Miscellany of Diverse Things*
and *All Roads Lead from Massilia*

"Mehler's *Bad is Bent Good* is a penetrating searchlight 360° of a dump site. The poetry doesn't descend into a fiery hell like Dante's *Inferno*, but there clearly **is** an inferno. The dump is a pitiless landscape of discarded machines, cardboard, rotted carcasses and dashed hopes. In this place there is a defiance in the air, a 'Fuck You' tattooed on the neck of a worker. No need for pity from whomever might be close enough to read it. Screw the lack of medical insurance, no hopes of job advancement, the low salaries. Like the poor everywhere, the marginalized, these workers will survive somehow.

"The workers recognize him as a longtime truckdriver, also a poet, who accepts their humanity, their humor and compassion for each other. *Bad is Bent Good* follows the men into their daily repetitive work in a landscape clouded with dust, but also brilliantly laid out against a pale blue sky at other times. I visualize seagulls flying around, and maybe a proud rat standing on a heap of rotted fruit. Did I get that from his poems, or is it the cumulative effect of the picture he constructs for us? He writes, *I clock in and leave the MRF building for the breakroom but pause to look up at the telephone wires. Dawn is breaking on a Saturday, and machines are still quiet, but perching and moving about on the wires is a colony of starlings that are setting up a roar of sound and activity.*

"The rhythm and style is plain, Middle-American, profound, suited for the subject at hand. He takes stock of the hard lives of the men at the dump, but also notes how two giant spiders in a jar are left to starve to death while the men eat their sandwiches unconcerned. He records this without overt judgment."

—Zeke Sanchez, author of *The Fire with Two Dragon Smokes: Before the Third Day*
and *Tiger Mountain: Hispanics in the Vietnam War*

"This is a book of faith, ultimately, exposing the reader, one encounter at a time, to the poet's vision of the Divine, and one character at a time, between high energy pulses like a quasar, noumenal to phenomenal, phenomenal to noumenal, and back again. Back and forth like that. Quicksilver. A deeply humane, frank, lyrical look at life, from a collection which has the intelligence and wisdom to reference scientific texts, education enough to quote Charles Simic, Czeslaw Milosz, Dante, Shakespeare, Borges, and the imagination to explore Jupiter and Europa, and to portray leviathans of the sea and the solar system, not necessarily in that order. All the while entreating God, how can he be of service. Begs to be set free. The ultimate anguish of what it means to be human. Many of these poems are dense narratives, long-lined, lengthy prose poems, which also happen to be intensely lyrical, mystical, and personal. The poems transmit metaphysical possibilities and frequently transcend this human plane of existence. What a magical place, the landfill. I will never experience a landfill as before, ever again. Everything is there, as the poet teaches us."

—Nancy Christopherson, author of *The Leaf* and *Topping Out*

"As Mehler explores this landfill terrain, so alien to most of us, the overlaps between poetry and rubbish/rejects here are endless to the last song. Punch lines build like an echo or a tide; a 'moral' spontaneously develops growing from the first line. Too often in poetry we see plain ordinary people of very little interest put on a pedestal, elevated at all costs and sold as some sort of mythical creatures occupied in very poetical businesses—none of this afflicts these characters: born in flesh and bones they go about the only way they can/know, part of the real world, cogs of the real struggle that clogs the streets of our neighborhood. There is nothing more real than the industry of getting rid of the rubbish that we produce.

"One question arises: is this poetry or a novel? Mehler could persuade us both ways. The overall perception is one of cohesion and resonance, and it's addictive. Try to picture a field: packed and whole when looked at from a distance; full of space, individuality and inimitability when approached closely. Elements of *Petits poèms en prose*, Baudelaire? Elements of *Small Moral Works*, Leopardi? Henry Chinasky could well be one of the boys who work the line. There is nothing fictional about these modern-day Argonauts traveling the furthest shores of a land(fill) that nobody this side of the world wants to confront. With nearly zero references on how they look, the more a reader's attention can be focused on the present moment conveyed and the more we are there amongst these characters. There is a sense of brittleness, inescapable, set under their skin, waiting to catch up with them, in their dreams, idiosyncrasies or random acts of rebellion or rituals performed as attempts to exorcize the madness that the day will bring. Money always comes into these stories as the needle of the scale, the ultimate arbiter, the divine grease that makes everything work and ties up, mopping up the little sense that life has to offer, the why, the how, the what which motivates bosses' actions, words and thoughts, the reason behind them carrying on breathing.

"The brilliance of these stories is in the numerous details that almost go unnoticed not because underplayed, but because treated with just the right level of attention, leaving the impression of looking at the world from another point of view, again, more real—which I find exquisite!"

—Massimo Fantuzzi, author of *Finizio, or The Alpha and Omega of Lester Aldridge*

Bad is Bent Good

poems

Dave Mehler

Aubade Publishing
Ashburn, VA

Copyright © 2025 Dave Mehler

All rights reserved. No part of this publication may be reproduced, stored in a retrieval system, or transmitted in any form or by any means, electronic, mechanical, photocopying, recording, or otherwise, without the prior written permission of Aubade Publishing.

Poems and fiction can be "actual" without being "factual." It is the author's belief that sometimes the actual can prove to be truer and more powerful (as distillations) than the factual, partly due to their reliance on story. Narrative (and poetry) can be truer than facts because they include emotions and layers of meaning which complete and integrate parts to form greater experiential wholes. These poems are actual rather than factual, even while some names have not been changed to honor my subjects. Everything written here, even when writing about myself, should never be construed to be factual, because all of it has been filtered, reinterpreted and amended through my observations, imagination, partiality, memory and finally through the act of writing in the medium of language for the purpose of making art and poetry out of life. Part of the author's goal as a poet is to bear witness and represent faithfully, but to the *actual* rather than the factual. The author's accounting of people and place in this work should not be taken literally.

Edited by Joe Puckett

Cover design and book layout by Cosette Puckett

Cover image reproduced from the painting *An Abundance of Caution* by Amy Casey

Library of Congress Control Number: 2025930444

ISBN: 978-1-951547-28-8

Published by Aubade Publishing, Ashburn, VA

Printed in the United States of America

To Mukhorty

For everyone will be salted with fire.

— **Mark 9:49**

If a book has anything to say, it burns with a quiet laugh, because any book worth its salt points up and out of itself.

— **Bohumil Hrabal, from *Too Loud a Solitude***

Table of Contents

One

2	Holiness of landfills
4	Selecting a reader
6	How to describe what's here? [I]
7	Ars Poetica, or, Explaining a book's utility to Pat, a non-reader

Two

10	A Logger, a Truck Driver and a Bow Hunter
11	Loyal
12	The new girl at the scale house
13	Lunchroom talk
14	Lunchroom table
16	Jimmy,
17	Shad
18	The Lazuli Bunting
19	Drift
20	I think of coal miners
21	Selling plasma
22	Bill
24	The Temp
25	Low-fat diet
26	Ragsdale said
27	The smelly bag of shit
28	Bad is bent good
29	Morning Break
30	Young banker
31	Vanity
32	Stored energy like a box of bullets some loose and rolling in the drawer
33	Treasure
34	Ignominy
35	Observation

Three

38	Cunningham relates a dream he had last night
39	Lion
40	Confession
41	Catfish
42	Clint used to be a cop.

43	A minor profundity regarding expediency versus shalom, Andrew
44	typed while standing in the porta-potty urinating just before clocking out on a Wednesday
45	We are daily witness to the world's wastes
46	Hobo
47	Cat's eye
48	Vectors
49	Drama
50	Movie
51	Deinonychus
52	Tainted meat and foolishness
54	As I was
55	*Think Green*
56	Randy
57	"13 acres
59	Pat describes an elk bugling
62	*Rattus rattus*
63	Amelia Earhart visits the landfill bearing a gift of wings
65	Considering buying a handgun,
66	Gun nuts
67	Rocky's story
68	When asked about tattooed wedding rings, Pat speaks words of welding:
69	I sit reading
71	Cunningham, spending an idle moment
72	Pond
73	Correspondence excerpt regarding Doug, the water truck driver
76	Travis 2, Temp mechanic

Four

78	The one God loves
81	Night owl
82	And the Lord said,
83	Nothing personal
84	Bizet
85	Protocluster
86	Sonny
87	Update from Dustin:
88	Leo
89	Mark
90	I wanted to interrupt
91	the meaning of the windshield in the previous poem
92	Owl in a box
93	Not empty

94	illuminated
95	Death of bowling and the various use of heads
96	Sleeping Dragonfly
97	Merton's teasels.
98	Rejoice, O Florence, since you are so great
99	Covered
101	A dry spell
102	Humming *Kokomo*
104	Overtime
106	Charles Hood on landfills, excerpted from an email
107	Europa
108	Being loaded
112	Pumping gas
113	Tim says,

Five

116	[II]
117	poetry fired in popcorn artillery bursts—
119	If it ain't got that
122	Landfill toys with eyes that watch
123	Dray Horse
124	Linked sonnets: *Absence like the sky, spread over everything—* and *Get Home Safe Every Day—*
125	Apparently there is a significant amount of trash on the moon:
126	Not even Little Blackie

Moonlights

130	Clint said
131	A record rain pouring down
132	*The white whale is not a symbol. He is as real as you or I.*
133	Rushing through the day to get to what matters
135	Rain Caps
136	Written on a Post-it by James, Oiler mechanic, and affixed to my bounced DVIR
138	Notes
140	Mini Glossary
141	Acknowledgements

One

If you're not breakin' shit, you ain't workin'

—Celorie dump truck driver

this shit I thumb-type into my phone comprises all my poetic output these days

It is only by labor that thought can be made healthy, and only by thought that labor can be made happy.

—John Ruskin

Holiness of landfills

Sparkling fiberglass insulation dust, I am some mother-of-pearl swirl
on the white hood of the Kenworth pulling out of the loading tunnel
into sudden stark sunshine. I devil up friable
dance toward windshield and lungs, pass through rolled down windows
into the hot airless cab to be pieces breathed-in wanting purchase, wanting to lodge.

God is the truck, driven, shifting and turning that climbs onto the scale. Workweary
hydraulic oil wept onto the platform which seeped past gaskets and seams drips off
hoses and overflows the reservoir vent cap is the LORD—I am the leak. Almighty
leviathan weighed overloaded always overweight passes by those who
wait in line heading the other way.

The Son is the two grey-striped kittens and the orange one, orphaned,
living in the drainage pipe under the scale that come out to play on the road
and bat at each other in harm's way. I am the scale attendant serving the public
in little more than underwear fainting from heatstroke because the AC

is on the fritz and I am also the rats that chewed through insulation and wiring
causing it to go out. The LORD is the heatwave and the sparrow chicks
too young to leave the nest which bake under the hot Spanish tile roof.

I am the view of Mt Hood from the wheelwash which rises up perfectly
in line with the truck exit seen when weather shines clear. God is the water spraying
from the bottom catchgrate and sidespouts baptizing truck wheels and undercarriage
free of mud and debris to keep the roads holy clear of trackout.

The Son is a 92-year-old man wearing a neckbrace bringing in a load
of yard debris, pine needles blackened resting in his trailer more than a year,
who jacknifes the trailer into his truck fender backing up to dump
because he can't turn his head. I am the employee who stops what he's doing

to help. God is the articulation of the off-road truck enabling it to turn so sharply
but I am the stiff spring under the seat that absorbs too little shock, and bumps
in the road pounding the driver's kidneys against an unforgiving seatback.

After the world is dumped on the tipping floor temp angels in and out of jail, wingshorn
they wear Hexarmor, hardhat and hi-vis PPE to sort and separate
the Elect from the Damned. Which are then weighed wanting. The Damned come
to me from tipping floor and from over the belt, each bearing their gilt and finely
wrought certificates of witness to destruction.

Prayer and petition carries us over the four channel radio, bouncing off a repeater
hidden somewhere, to then be trucked up haul road to tipper and dozed,
compacted—buried—God the belly of the trailer which bears it
and I the sounds of fingernails clawing inside metal walls
after it reaches tipping point and the door opens (forever)

because the Angel of the LORD's thumb pushes the RAISE button lifting
a groaning deck. I am the joystick
which causes the excavator cab of the Hitachi 300 to swing
and the Father the swingbrake which stops it from swinging.
The LORD is boom and stick and mighty fist of the great-toothed bucket

opening and closing working the stiff-necked trash out stuck fast
on cross-members—charging for dig-out when it refuses to slide—
jammed up with phone poles or plastic pipe exploding into shrapnel—

I am waste, indwelt, truck tabernacled, Father and Son is the management,
the devil is the kill switch pulled after hauling load after load of cover
dirt to the top of the fill—this ends a running engine.

I am the methane that collects at the bottom of the cell piped to a flare
to be burned off and the Son is the circle of birds
whose feather-singed bodies gather at the base as burnt
free-will offerings flown through invisible flame, who is the Spirit,
blue-hued appearing only at night, only before sunrise,

only between dusk and dawn during the nightfall's sabbath
before the new day's hot work begins.

Selecting a reader

for Dustin Hartford

Let him be a heavy equipment operator,
with some college,
who double-majored in anthropology and non-western religions,
but not a reader per se.

Have him be an employee at a landfill, someone deeply acquainted with tedium
but uncomplaining, perhaps even content, let him work
someplace in old, tired, broken-down equipment
where skill is optional finesse not required,
where he is encouraged to be stoic about boredom
and enjoys the stability, and excellent vacation benefits.

Let him own a Harley and go to Sturgis religiously in late summer.
Do pub crawls with co-workers on weekends,
kayak the ocean between the San Juan's camping out with his brother.

Let him be one who never marries
and a man of little or no ambition, but a generous uncle
who spends a small fortune taking niece and nephew to Disneyland.
Let him visit his girlfriend who lives on the dry side of the state
driving out to see her in Prineville nearly every weekend,
for years.

In stature let him be smallish
but no wimp. Not an outdoorsman, because he was raised by a husbandless
mother who owns a quilt store in Tillamook and is vegan, but

not afraid to wander off on an adventure and contend
alone in the wilderness. Have him bicycle
cross-country camping and sleeping in ditches,
and find *this* fun.

But never ever let it ever occur to him to do like you did
(even after reading about it) and drive long-haul
sleeping and eating out of his truck,
while getting paid to do so. Let him

find your book incidentally,
given him almost as an afterthought—
but he will be immediately interested, only because
you wrote it—let him take it home

to read it in a single night!
Cover to cover—then come in next morning
to report to you the four he liked best explaining casually slow,
but articulately,
why.
And then, let him
proceed to press the book on mother, brother, girlfriend.

Yours will be the first
and the last poetry book he'll ever read.
Not because he didn't like it
but because he will never come across
another living poet.

Let him forever be
this enigma.

How to describe what's here? [I]

Rejects all
unloved, the ugly unwanted,
the dumped and discarded sun still shines on for now,
conceived in haste tasteless these
bad ideas borne out of poverty of imagination
or production somehow purchased
reconsidered then someway seen with fresher clearer eyes
to be useless, outlived or outstripped, obsolete
the unlovely and finally forsaken ending here, also
the once loved fractured, fragmented worn-out
disgusted, the hauled off and off-putting, the dragged away screaming,
decidedly unredeemed not even God wants anything to do with,
things that don't or never worked right, the unsalvageable,
poor by design, the belligerent drunk and schematized obsolescence,
hoses with holes,
bellies distended and jobless,
the mostly unskilled inhabiting barstools asap after clocking out,
the mouthing obscenities all day long as we work up to
and including the articulate who know better,
the picked through not picking through and deemed non-recyclable,
the damaged by association, unrequited, illiterate, the snaggle-toothed
meth-heads who fix the broken equipment ensuring it just barely does
or will work another hour,
the crumpled, patched, mounded and piled then compacted
crushed by sheepsfoot with heavy steel-cleated wheels
blunted but still protruding whose job
to depress what bounces back till it doesn't bounce
back, the puncturing and relieving of air and volume, prepping
for cover dirt (deep enough to prevent maggots). Also
the duct-taped dropped on the road and blown away on the way to burial.
What sticks to the trailer door hanging by a flap or snagged by a bolt thread
wire wrapped around a wheel between duals. All that ire
most stubborn most deserving. Scary rubbish poisonous
unidentifiable. Tiny hidden invisibly slow killers
breathing or imbibed,
and occasional beauty seen or thought,
not ever voiced, not ever heard. The uncanniness
of pleasant smells and any worry that might incite. Birds flying
around—everywhere—, including the bird hired
to kill or drive them off.

Ars Poetica, or, Explaining a book's utility to Pat, a non-reader

Books are power tools
poems are toys
or vehicles, also a gun

Two

I think also that, could I start anew, every poem of mine would have been a biography or a portrait of a particular person, or in fact, a lament over his or her destiny.

–Czeslaw Milosz, from *Pity*

Travis, I don't think I'm going to make it. I love you.

–Voicemail from a temp mechanic's father, aged 52, left during his massive coronary

Send whiskey and fresh horses

–George Washington

A Logger, a Truck Driver and a Bow Hunter

Sitting in the breakroom one of us noted Cunningham was gone and off hunting in the coast range while an ice storm and cold front was moving in. I think it was me who said then, I wouldn't mind being at the coast right now. Both Ryan and Pat echoed that refrain. Ryan wished he was back in the woods logging, said, A young man's game, but I still miss it. Pat said, I'd love nothing better than to be hunting elk in woods knee-deep in snow. He said this with a smile, looking wistful, away, to take himself there. Then, Well not in the middle of a blizzard. I said, I'm surprised tags are available this time of year. He said, Oh yeah, you can get tags for February, the problem is cows are usually pregnant. Some hunters refuse to hunt this time of year because of that. I don't have a problem with it, but some do. Then, Actually, my kids have gotten tags for does, and it is difficult explaining.

I think about two instead of one, I think about the sharp knife going in and a calf curled up coming out along with the entrails slick and asleep eyes that never opened, never licked into breathing, or a fawn suffocating inside the darkness of a womb after the blood stops pumping not knowing what's happening suddenly to the stopping of life stopped, the trauma beginning then ebbing as the dark angels with guns make their approach. Finally, the plop of blood and guts melting snow. Is it my softness or his hardness, and whose or what lack? Each? Given provocation and threat Pat would commit violence and die fiercely to protect his calf. I can tell he is aware of all this as he said it but has gone past it or trained it out of himself. He pauses, maybe seeing what I imperfectly imagine, remembering the visuals? Then he says again, It's difficult to explain the why to your kids. Some people have a hard time with it. I say, I know I would. And he says, Yeah, yeah many do.

This is the damage he does me, this morning, still
dark, freezing rain falling as we three sit sipping
shitty Folger's coffee with heat but no flavor.

Loyal

He shows up Monday morning with blood red knuckles on his right hand from punching something and we exchange a look—

"Rough weekend?" I say, and his response, "Yeah, sometimes I reach a point I'm not proud of, when things just get to be too much."

He has sworn off kids even though his wife wants them, because his father was an older man with high standards and little patience, who beat him. He refuses to be placed in a position of repeating that cycle, fearful he might, after watching other parents raising their children around him. He knows more about the machinery and maintains a more professional attitude than any other mechanic I've seen come and go through this shop.

The new girl at the scale house

I haven't yet learned her name but I still know something about her and what she loves.
In Portland we wear adornments on our arms our very hearts on sleeves.

Little splashes of neon lavender, hot pink, chartreuse.
A little red and yellow and black, blotched colors to complement each design.

A stylized bumblebee below, monarch caterpillar to the side,
and a ladybug above, made to look *chibi*, except the caterpillar doesn't come off

—is too literally larval and pointy. The composition suffers—makes it
monstrous. Images look fuzzy, applied with pastels rather than ink.

Hired around Fourth of July; her fingernails alternated red, white and blue.

She wears no rings. And may never. Today an uncommemorated day mid-August
her nails alternate white, hot pink and a lighter shade of orange sherbet

like a sky at twilight, warm amber that so sweetly lingers and mellows to peach
once the sun has set, so perfect in fall, before greying to purple then

when the soft streetlights blink on
and a heat still emanates from sidewalks and street.

Soon the moon, and crickets will chirp,
an owl in the nearby grand old oak may lift off

or call out the dusk. Hungry for dark to settle in, and to greet the night.

Lunchroom talk

Talk of dead or dying friends comes up because Ron has a friend dying of lung cancer. Terry mentions someone he knew who didn't smoke or chew, always ate healthy and exercised, but died in his early forties of stomach cancer. "You never can tell," he says. Unspoken but on everyone's mind, including Terry's, is that he's 63 and has smoked hard for over 40 years. Terry says, "I'll just keep working till my health takes a shit." Cunningham, double-dipping with smokes and chew and not quite forty, says, "I hope it's by the Wilson, and I slip on some slick rocks, and slide into a deep, green pool."

Lunchroom table

Besides the catalogs for used cars and trucks, tools, and heavy equipment, there is a brochure for Leupold scopes, an Oregon Big Game Hunting Regulations booklet, a Portland Street Guide and a color printout of a hunter someone knows holding up off the ground embraced in a bearhug a wolf of prehistoric proportions. The sagging, grey muzzled head, eyes closed at peace, dwarfs the tanned melon head of the hunter strained, peeking around the neck and over the huge foreleg and paw of the wolf, its tail and back legs touch the straw-colored ground of the clearing in front of a backdrop of ponderosas. A note written in the blue sky between the treetops, "Drayton Valley, Alberta, 230 lb. wolf."

Courtesy of Ron, head shop mechanic, are five photocopies of internet photographs in a pile on the table. The first depicts a game warden with an Ohio wildlife shoulder patch kneeling above three severed buck heads, their horns locked but tie-wrapped to ensure they don't slip apart, the ground littered with leaves, bare trees in the background. The second shows three headless bucks lined up and lying on the ground, detached heads in the foreground, the deer on the right lies with legs and hooves laying over the back of the buck in the middle, and four men kneel behind posing for the picture while another stands behind them, frowning, cap bill low over the brow—the one kneeling on the right smiles and wears long rubber gloves and waders. The third photo is similar to the first except that in this photo the ranger smiles down at the camera which is at ground level and even with the dead buck's antler-tangled, hide-matted heads. The fourth shows the three heads, locked horns, cut or sawn from the bodies and lying half on the truck bed and half on the tailgate of the ranger's pickup. The fifth picture, as if gone backward in time, shows the three bucks floating in the river, drowned bodies pointing outward like three rays from a central point, resembling a geometric word problem, or skydivers who've joined hands falling through sky toward earth. Many elongated pointed maple leaves float on the surface of the still water near the corpses, tiny boats that resemble antlers.

These black and white photocopies somehow bring to mind a recent news story about a rescue operation of a female humpback whale tangled up in crab pots near the Farallon Islands, a few miles off the coast of San Francisco. A fishing boat crew reported seeing the immobilized whale on the verge of drowning. They called in the coordinates to some environmental agency, who then sent out a boat full of foolhardy good Samaritan divers. They assessed and finally approached the whale with curved knives even after she tried to warn the boat away with her one free fifteen-foot-long flipper. The tail was underwater weighted down by at least twenty crab pot traps—each pot weighing approximately 90 pounds and each attached to two hundred and forty feet of line, with weights every sixty feet. The whale floating like a question mark, line wrapped around her body through her mouth and over her eye, cutting through to blubber, she struggled to keep her blowhole above water. The divers didn't think they could save her but swam close enough to begin cutting through the lines, into and under the skin to free her. After an hour they finished, and after they were done, she swam in circles around them, coming back to nudge the shoulder or chest, making eye contact with each, and lingering for minutes. What does any of this signify? Would somebody please—anyone—care to explain this to me, please?

Jimmy,

the operator everyone hates because he has done everything and knows it all already while daily demonstrating he doesn't, is building an identity in narrative with ink on his skin like a suit of armor. He shows me a bear paw print on his right inner bicep still a raw pink and fresh, "fierce if provoked;" and praying skeleton hands, "don't judge me;" the face of a large wolf on his forearm, "gentle giant." He has a friend who has spent countless hours on him and they barter work and favors or he'd never be able to afford this. He tells me he has plans for many more images from nature. Until he becomes subsumed in myth and self-deception that explain and show who he'd like to be and how he wishes to be seen. But I caught the look of rage on his face one day when a co-worker in the breakroom warned him that he knew Jimmy's girlfriend had been visiting her old flame in prison and hiding it from him. In less than an instant all those tattoos became meaningless.

Shad

As we discussed Jimmy's tattoos while eating lunch in the breakroom, I happened to notice three dots of old ink which formed an inverted triangle on the web of skin between thumb and forefinger on his left hand. I asked, "Is that a tattoo?" and he said, "Yes, but it's not the way you think. When I was six, I took a sewing needle and did it myself. I was going for a smiley face but it hurt so much, I stopped after the eyes and nose."

The Lazuli Bunting

Such a smart blue sight at the landfill flitting iridescent over the dry dead stalks which stand cold and hollow over the newer green growth. Color like the blue brushes, dismantled pieces from a carwash demo, and sudden bundles of blue hairnets and neoprene gloves falling loosely to land here and there dotting the concrete, or the calm steady appearance of blue caused by Rayleigh scattering doppled a bluer blue above under this high-pressure zone of sky which just is.

Drift

"I'd love to row down the Trask. Throw in a couple of quickfish on either side. Let them trail behind, then anchor up, and cast out bobber and eggs into the holes. Trailing quickfish drifting down the Trask, float out bobber and eggs. That'd be funner than shit." Cunningham had a look of wonder on his face as though he were peering into an illuminated manuscript as he said this.

"I got a drift boat," Terry says, "and it's even got an outboard."

I think of coal miners

The people who work the line and sort what's fed over the moving conveyer belt pick out the recyclable material and throw it down holes to the boxes below and let the leftover trash stream by untouched. These are hired through a temp agency called Labor Ready. The advantage to the temp worker in doing this work (besides a paycheck) is that some of the better more dependable workers have an opportunity to work their way into full-time operator positions as the need arises. This has happened five or six times in the last year. First, they supervise the line, then they might run a loader, work as a load inspector, or in the shop, or manage the Z-wall. In this way the corporation can try them out, risk free, keep only the best, have them come in one day and not the next. But most of them don't get full-time hours, and are middle-aged, unskilled laborers, men and women. The cops showed up one day looking for one who attacked and put his roommate in the hospital the night before because he wanted sleep but his roommate wouldn't stop partying. Living in half-way houses, in and out of jail, getting into bar fights, and between real jobs, walking, biking, riding the bus, or carpooling to work five or six with one of the four who owns and can afford a car. But working, working the line in all the decibels and dust, whether it's a hundred or twenty degrees, they're holding down a job. All of them smoke, and the work they do is dirty, dizzying, and hard, a bottom rung without status. I see them and think of coal miners. They have their own lunchroom and safety meetings but occasionally the line workers and operators have a joint meeting and there are twelve to fifteen of them. One sits down to my right, pulls a sandwich from a baggie, and there tattooed on the left side of his neck, two words in ornate script: *fuck you*.

Selling plasma

Kyle used to work the line but now he helps out in the shop, changing oil or tires or using the firehose on the water truck to clean the tracks on dozers. He takes a break in the lunchroom now, noting everyone's salad, but not eating. At first, I worry he had to go without a lunch today, but he points to the empty Tupperware on the table in front of him. We all talk about losing weight and the struggle to keep to our diets. Tall and lanky and still young, he says he has to start staying away from bacon. Back when he was selling plasma before he moved in with his sister who feeds him balanced healthy food he says, you could see the fat in your blood as they filtered it out into a receptacle. It was gross. I asked him how often you could sell blood and how much you could get for it. They pay fifty bucks, and you can sell it up to twice a week. They take 35 ounces. Damn, that's a large soda at 7-Eleven, I said. Yeah, and you should see the size of the needle—bigger than the tip on this ballpoint. Feels great, and it takes close to an hour. They use a machine to take the blood cells out of the plasma and then put them back into you. You got to be sure not to drink for at least an hour afterward, or smoke—and he motions toward the table smacking it with his hand—but it's pretty funny to see the people who do. You can always tell.

Bill

As the west-side loader operator for the MRF, Bill always finds himself between two orders of wrath because it's up to him to decide where to push the loads that are dropped on the floor by incoming trucks. He can push it to Claudio where it will end up in my trailer or he can push it to Troy where it will be fed over the line for sorters to pick from. One or the other of them is constantly berating him over the radio for his decisions: If Claudio, for getting lots of recyclables like wood and metal, or Troy, for getting fluffy residual that hangs up and clogs the conveyor end. I think Bill's biggest problem is he's not very bright, but he's at least bright enough to be stressed all the time. I truly believe he's trying. Claudio believes he's self-centered and does what suits him, which is to expend the least effort, and has nicknamed him Bildo. Cunningham, the foreman, claims that Bill's job is the most stressful job in the building and cites that he never ever complains about it.

As the loader operator he comes in early like Claudio and I, and will sometimes share events of the previous night, like going to the bar where a woman had a fake boob and invited others to touch it. Or the time he was taking home a homeless, female line worker who put his declawed, indoor cat out, and he didn't realize it until the cat was making loud noises throwing itself at the sliding glass door to get back in. The cat may very well have been in mortal danger from coyotes or a cougar. The way Bill talked, he and the line worker were sleeping in separate rooms and he was taking her in as a favor because she had nowhere else to go, but of course we suspected different motives, whether sex or just loneliness. After her disordered life became too much to handle, he was done helping her.

Bill started out on the line as a temp, had been recently divorced, and was living with his mother. He was probably in his mid-forties then. After he got promoted to operator, his mother and aunt found a doublewide just inland from the coast in Otis, a town that had been for sale and included a cafe and a gas station, so he moved into a place closer to work, a little cabin in the foothills this side of the Coast Range. Bill wears wire rim glasses and is wiry and thin, but somehow still manages to have a pouchy belly. He is a compulsive gambler, going to casinos, talking about wins off scratch tickets, and smoking heavily. At some point he started buying new cars, first a Hummer, then an F350 truck, and finally a Jeep Cherokee—he would trade them in each time at a loss, and then have to tell us all about it. He couldn't grasp how painful this might be to watch.

Then one day he hooked up with a girl working on the line, 20 years younger and a Latina who looked half his age, was attractive, and had barrio tats. Pretty soon she became known as Bill's girlfriend. They drove in together, ate lunch together, lived together, and for a while it seemed Bill was trying to clean up his act: he ate better, quit drinking, smoked less as if the fact that someone cared about him was giving him a reason to live—permission to give a shit about himself.

They seemed—to watch him—in love—and we were waiting to hear they'd gotten married, when Bill announced they were taking a trip to Vegas to gamble and to meet her parents. It turned out to be the same weekend the concert outside the MGM Grand got shot up by some kook from Mesquite. They were blocks away when it happened, and it wasn't too long after that things started to unravel. Bill started to get skinnier. We began wondering if he'd slipped into meth use or a crack pipe—because he was no longer just skinny—he began looking gaunt— noticeably enough for co-workers to remark on it and speculate. Then one day he started wearing his hoodie with the hood up and this went on for several days. Andrew spoke to him about it in the breakroom one morning and he overreacted by saying, "I'm wearing the hood up because I had an accident and didn't want everyone looking at it, okay!? Now you know!"

Maybe a couple weeks later, he came in Monday, Dustin was sitting with his back to him, and Claudio and I were in our usual chairs, and he said it was over. He'd called the cops on her. She had been abusing him for four months, then this weekend she punched him and broke his glasses, and he showed us the swelling under his eye, and she had nearly killed him while they were in the car at a McDonalds. With superhuman strength she reached over and strangled him into unconsciousness. "I'm a strong guy," he said, "but I couldn't get her off me. The next thing you know, I wake up and look and she's outside the window looking in at me, laughing. I called the cops on her, and they came and picked her up. Domestic violence." No one wanted to look at him as he said all this. Finally, I said, "Wow, Bill, I'm really sorry to hear that." Then a bit later that morning I was seeing him drive off. Claudio said he thought he'd be heading to the jail to bail her out.

About a month later, he moved into a new apartment in Tigard, and news got around she'd be moving back in with him. I told him he was being a fool but all he did was look at me stony-faced, knowing it was true, but wanting what he wanted, planning to do it anyway. I can't stand it when Claudio turns out to be right, out of pure hatefulness, but nailing it. He gave his two weeks, quit and moved down to Arizona with her, no job prospects, which suggested it was her idea and he was just following her down there.

Then, after four or five years we heard from Cunningham he was getting rehired. He even hailed a greeting to me over the radio, but I didn't respond, hardly knowing what to say. Uniform materials showed up in the break room in his size with his name on them, waiting for him. Days passed, no Bill. Finally, I asked, "Where's Bill?"—Failed his drug screen, won't be returning—

The Temp

Someone's always teasing the new kid, Josh—making fun of his inexperience in life and work—he's got braces and his grandmother packs his lunch. He just smiles or laughs it off, which is the perfect response. He got hired because he's a family friend of Ragsdale's and they both volunteer for the Banks Fire Dept. Ragsdale shakes him down every day for the peanut butter cups his grandmother packs in his lunches. One day, sitting around the table in the lunchroom, Cunningham asked, "You're 18, aren't you? Shit! To be eighteen again." Everyone reflected for a moment, nodding, except me. Ragsdale said, "I wouldn't be married . . ." Cunningham said, "I'd go to college." Scott, the angry dozer operator, who's henpecked and comes to work early to get away from a house full of noisy grandkids in diapers said, "I'd be in Afghanistan."

Low-fat diet

Ragsdale, pushing 43, offers up the results of his stress test; everything looked good except for his liver enzymes, so they want him to go on a low-fat diet. This doesn't explain the two breakfast sandwiches he's eating. Then at breaktime, pink frosted pop tarts with multi-colored sprinkles and a Rockstar energy drink. Hey Ragsdale, just out of curiosity, what did you have for dinner last night? A couple of quarter pounders. You went to McDonalds? Holy crap, dude! This was all in celebration at the news nothing worse was wrong, and because he didn't have time to make dinner. The next morning I was relieved to see him eating a chocolate and vanilla pudding cup.

Ragsdale said

I almost wished I woulda did that

The smelly bag of shit

Ragsdale was telling me that yesterday he found a bag of HUMAN SHIT while in his hoe, sorting—it got everywhere. Who keeps and then throws away a garbage bag full of shit? he wanted to know. So he tracked over to Leo and said Leo I gotta tell you something. Leo opened the door of the 644 to see what he wanted and Ragsdale slid the boom over, wagging his dripping bucket next to the door and watched Leo gag. He was telling us all this at lunch time and laughing. How did you know it was human? I wanted to know. The bite of sandwich he'd been chewing came out of his mouth.

Bad is bent good

Alan and I developed a competitive morning ritual of trading strange news stories. I think he must surf the net doing research every night beforehand. There was the man in Florida who loses a hand to an alligator only to be fined for feeding alligators. The woman charging for fake Botox injections, finally having the law catch up with her after a parade of victims, horrendously deformed in butt cheeks and face, filed suit because she was injecting them with combinations of happy things like super glue, fix-a-flat, drywall mud. Or how fourth of July in San Diego at the bay the big fireworks show went off in 9 seconds flat, 30 minutes before the scheduled time instead of the hour long show that had been planned.

This morning he tells me of a quarry in Germany known more for unearthed fossil treasures than the rock that was originally mined there. Most recently a discovery was made of a pair of 50-million-year-old turtles, joined eternally, frozen in coitus. It is supposed they were drifting into the depths in the midst of this activity and hit a pocket of toxic gasses.

Morning Break

During a morning break, BBQ Bob, the district shop manager, was passing through the lunchroom on his way back from the shop to his office and came over to Cunningham, says, holding a pair of safety glasses, We just had another eye injury back east, but this time the employee was wearing his safety glasses. The projectile came over the top and behind the frame to enter the eye. We really have to watch and take special care when folks are using grinders or sanding and sparks or debris start flying. He's still in the hospital and they don't know if they'll be able to save it. Imagine trying to do your job, or find other work in your field with a handicap like that? After he left, I told Cunningham, This reminds me of the meltdown in Japan at the Fukushima plant. Why? Cunningham asked. Well, here we are worrying about wearing safety glasses to the point where you're fricking wearing them in the lunchroom, for fear of a peanut butter and jelly sandwich, while they're over there flooding a reactor with sea water to cool it down after cooling failure, an 8.9 earthquake, a tsunami, radiation leaks and fallout with little or no infrastructure left to deal with it. Do you imagine the workers over there madly trying to contain that mess or clean it up making certain first, and only then, they have their safety glasses on!?

I say this because I hate Bob, but Cunningham ignores that and looks over at me as if I've just become a source of the latest news. What's going on in Libya? We just started bombing the fuck out of everything yesterday, Randy says.

Young banker

A driver for Allied Waste brings in permitted loads direct to the landfill; blue trucks in a doubles rig, hauling drop boxes out of Wilsonville. This morning he steps down out of the cab of his roll-off truck and walks to the back—he walks out of his way to kick a stuffed bear lying on the pad. This driver is fat in a soft pudgy way, not the kind of overweight with muscle underneath but the kind that never knew any muscle or hardness. He wears spectacles and resembles the stuffed bear, and when spoken to, replies in an Alabama country boy accent, which surprises because he should sound like a young banker or lawyer who decided to get his hands dirty for a day. After raising the boom, dumping the contents out of the box and resecuring the doors, he kicks it again, this time harder.

Vanity

The Greenway driver is a retired longshoreman but doesn't look a day over fifty. He likes to wear T-shirts without sleeves so that they show off his muscular biceps. His short silver hair, combed back, and the mustache which grows down below the bottom lip, are neatly trimmed. He has a story for each of us: His house in San Diego, or a place on the Big Island. He doesn't need this job but his girlfriend has kids in the area she doesn't want to leave behind, and he's just helping out Terence by running this route. After I tip his trailer, but before he backs up onto the platform to rehook to the trailer, he takes a second to dump out a full ashtray on the ground. After he's gone and I walk past the pile of butts, I notice every cigarette has been smoked down to the filter. This tells me far more than everything I need to know.

Stored energy like a box of bullets some loose and rolling in the drawer

The morning always begins in the breakroom with Ragsdale eating little cakes covered with white icing or pop tarts with rainbow sprinkles, only this morning he announces, "Shari says the kids'll be out of the house tonight, so I guess I'll be getting some. Married eighteen years and she still puts up with me." Scott says, "If that were my house, it would be, 'the kids are going to be out of the house tonight and I want you gone too.' I haven't had sex for twelve years—it's not so bad once you get through the withdrawals." Ragsdale says, "So that's why you're angry all the time. I'd be spending a lot of time at Peeps."

At Stimson, the place Cunningham worked as foreman before this job, a millwright was killed and two others were injured after a hydraulic accumulator exploded. Cunningham told us, after he'd gotten the call that he had worked with these men and knew them personally, and the man who died had thirty or forty years at the mill and would have retired but continued working to maintain health benefits for his ailing wife. No one knew what had gone wrong yet, but he told us the hydraulic cylinder had lifted the press millions of times over the course of its life, and the only reason for millwrights to be hanging around the accumulator would be if it was acting up and they were trying to troubleshoot it. Several times he paused, eyes watering, before he could speak again. Part of him had to be very relieved this hadn't happened on his watch.

I pulled onto the scale and sparrows were flapping and rolling over the dusty asphalt, fighting beak to beak. At first I thought maybe the struggle was sexual, "They're humping," I said, "No," Andrew said, "it's a fight." One on its back and the other wouldn't let go of his beak, then they shot straight up into the air scratching at each other with their feet, beaks still attached, then fell and broke off, one fleeing and the other pursuing to a plum tree twenty-five yards away. Even the meek are fierce with each other, and to witness such things seems more an aberration than alligators eating their young, who sing just before hatching.

Treasure

People constantly forget, or they never knew. Valuables get mixed in with trash or get accidentally left behind near the dump site. Later, discovering their mistake they call or come back panicked to see if anyone found the object. Usually, it's a wallet or a cellphone or some variety of tool. The scale calls over the radio that someone is going to come over and look around. They insist on inspecting the area themselves around the 53-yard box or the pile that's been pushed up already by a bucket loader. It's all part of the grieving process, and mistrust. A gold coin collection in a wooden box that wasn't supposed to be tossed. A wedding ring that slipped off the finger into a glove that got left behind. A priceless comic book or sports card collection. You can call the cellphone you just left behind a second ago and it's so far gone already you'd never hear even a muffled ring. It might just as well have passed into the Underworld. But then at some point, the item may resurface momentarily before human eyes again to go across the line: A file cabinet drawer pops open and a file folder full of twenties flies out, or more commonly it's sharps in the form of a diabetic's dirty needle repository that splits open and scatters biohazard from a broken milk jug, or a decomposing pet python passes by. Or someone turns up a tossed murder weapon then as a joke aims it sideways, gangsta-style, at the poor jackass sorting across from him, accidentally discharging a round.

Ignominy

The economy went through the guardrails that night on Mulholland with multiple Madoffs at the wheel; a couple jumped clear with bonuses, another slipped out those snazzy suicide doors in a tux clutching a parachute. Some remained trapped wearing seatbelts as the ragtop rolled and rolled over rocks and scrub finally flipping one last time to rest upside down, gas dripping—pre-explosion—but the mad back wheels keep spinning without purchase, as if a foot still floors the accelerator because it was in the interests of government to keep them solvent to continue to eat each other and us a while longer. That's when we started seeing Jacuzzis at the landfill come in by the truckload, individually or five and six at a time on a flatbed, old sportsmans' boats too, and RVs the owner could no longer afford to pay to gas up or park in storage, and not even a fool would buy. The trackhoe just punched and pieced them up like stale prosperity, or folds them up like empty billfolds, scrap metal trucked across the river to WA to be barged in a box overseas to China to build more ghost malls, the rest going in my trailer to head up the hill for burial.

Observation

I clock in and leave the MRF building for the breakroom but pause to look up at the telephone wires. Dawn is breaking on a Saturday, the machines are still quiet, but perching and moving about on the wires is a colony of starlings that are setting up a roar of sound and activity. The level of sound underneath is short clicks and sharp chirps that most of the birds are making. Away from the middle of the lines, toward the pole and transformer, some are croaking and scratching extended songs in recursion, and these are louder. Some birds fly from one spot to another part of the line, and whenever they do this, they pick a gap of wire to land, and the birds on either side sidle a bit making room. Some perch closer than others, but there is a mean of a birdwidth plus a half. It's not easy to estimate but there must be close to a hundred birds, some of which are starlings, and some blackbirds. One bird will be dangling by its feet below the line and others will be pecking at it until it drops flying away, but nothing violent, just seemingly out of mild annoyance or a harmless poking fun. This happens a few times. Then one bird will look at the bird next to it, and they will shift, closing in or increasing the gap. They flutter wings and fidget, each one so full of movement, sound, and flight. There is too much social activity for it to be taken in all at once. One must move one's gaze from one set to another set of individuals. Twice, as a group, the birds collectively flinch and when they do this, they go silent momentarily. There was no apparent reason for this, either time. And then a group from the landing of the landfill flies in as a cloud to line up on the empty wires next to the first group. Not long after this the first group flies and reorganizes on the other side of the birds who've just arrived. They are like tiny black, feathered people, mostly extended family, interacting with one another. Filled with wonder, I watched all this as though carefully unwrapping and enjoying a favorite piece of candy. I take a minute and try to imagine how the Hemingway of *Cat in the Rain* might begin a description of this observation. Then, I wonder about the surveillance cameras and the recording loop and speculate what anyone in Houston or Dale arriving soon on site might make of this caught on video, me standing in the road transfixed, looking up for so many minutes at what appears to be absolutely nothing at all.

Three

Maybe dullness is associated with psychic pain, because something that's dull or opaque fails to provide enough stimulation to distract people from some other, deeper type of pain that is always there, if only in an ambient low-level way, and which most of us spend nearly all our time and energy trying to distract ourselves from.

–David Foster Wallace, from *The Pale King*

We have strong feelings about bulldozers, their buzzing and scraping, their clumsy abruptness, their way of tipping saplings into burnable roots and brush. Our faces get vinegary when we think of it. But the bulldozer's point of view is remarkably different. The bulldozer thinks of itself as a lover.

–David Young, from *Four about Heavy Machinery*

Descartes, I hear, did his best philosophizing by lazing in bed past noon. Not me! I'm on my way to the dump tooting my horn and waving to the neighbors.

–Charles Simic, from *The Monster Loves his Labyrinth: Notebooks*

Cunningham relates a dream he had last night

"After work I took a walk with my daughter in the woods behind our house. On the way back I could see deer prints inside my prints and I showed them to her, then a little bit further on there were cat prints over those and I started to get a little worried. We got back to the house and I grabbed my pistol and headed out to the back porch and the cougar was there staring at me. I took aim, but I couldn't get it to work." He motions with his hands clasped like he's aiming a pistol and shaking it around, looking at his hands, frustrated. "Finally, I got one off and hit the cat in the nose, and it was bleeding down its face, so I knew I hit it, but it just kept standing there in the yard staring me down. I tried to shoot it again to kill it but the pistol wouldn't fire. Then I woke up, thinking, damn, I didn't get my cat." Then he laughed and said, "I often have fishing dreams that are frustrating like that where I'm having a great fight with a chinook, then twang, and it's gone." I could see this last part was covering up something that had been shown and then quickly hidden, something about young daughters. Footprints within prints. Guns that won't fire and fierce creatures that can't or won't die.

Lion

I'm not afraid of bears, but cats — they're killers —

—**Pat Sargent**

One morning before dawn, I was driving down from the fill and I saw two of them run across the road in front of me to get into the weedy area behind the Z-wall. One looked back—I could see it was ginger-colored and striped. Smaller but stockier than a chihuahua, it looked like it had a mane, and was trying to roar at me. Another day I startled them and they ran out of the tunnel as I was heading down in. I mentioned this to the Z-wall attendant, Alan, who just had a baby daughter, and the miracle of this was causing him to consider no longer having a sixpack after work every night, and he said, "Yeah, I've been finding parts of kittens everywhere. One got flattened and I found it after I moved the forklift, and over by box 12, I found a set of paws—just the paws! Over by the shingle box a pile of guts. There are many things around this landfill that find kittens make good eating."

Confession

Cunningham confessed to us that he captured a neighborhood cat that had been coming into his home through the cat door to eat his cat's food. He put it in a box and drove it to work the next day, then released it at the landfill, ten miles away from his home in Forest Grove. After a woman posted signs with a picture of Oliver, Lost Cat, and wandered the neighborhood night after night calling him, Cunningham felt guilty and decided to try to locate the cat in order to return him. Brad thought it had probably ended up in the barn at the house onsite he rents, which is full of cats. Cunningham would show up each morning trying to lure him out and was sure he'd sighted him in front of the barn hanging out with the other cats. Even when called, Oliver wouldn't come near him though, and disappeared whenever he showed any sign of approaching. Rigging a cage to trap him with raw meat did no good. It appeared Oliver had found his people finally and was quite satisfied with his new home.

Catfish

About once a week if I don't wash down the approach and exit to the tunnel, the dust, an amalgamation of drywall, fiberglass powder, dirt, insulation and wood products, starts to build up where driving through the tunnel stirs up clouds and loading trailers creates clouds and I'm breathing the stuff in all day long and I can feel my lungs full of it all in the shortness of breath reminiscent of a two pack a day habit. So, I get in the water truck and drive over to the pond and load it. At the end of summer, the pond gets low since it hasn't been raining much and we use more water to keep the dust down on the unpaved roads around the site and wet down the feed pile in the MRF to manage the dust, so inevitably the pump pumps fish into the truck tank. When you spray down the road or a tunnel the evidence of heads, tails and whole catfish are everywhere. The opening on the sprayer spouts are relatively narrow slits to make the spray easier to direct. Some of the fish that come out whole are amazing considering the opening they were forced through, but most of them are mangled and torn up into pieces. Some must have been small enough to have navigated the pump and the sprayer head and lain there gasping for air for some time. One thing learned from all this is that catfish have blood, but not much—you can see it in the color of the guts, but not much else. After spraying down both ends of the tunnel, fish parts and carcasses are everywhere. I wondered if I should shovel them up in case it started to smell, but then I remembered the kittens, so I waited. Sure enough, night after night they began disappearing—finally, the only thing left, kitten paw prints in the dusty walkway, and whiskered fish heads, the only thing they wouldn't eat.

Clint used to be a cop.

Maybe that's why he keeps going around trying to save everyone. His beat was in Carlton, and I asked him one day how he ended up here. He said, Oh didn't you hear the story, and then proceeded to tell it again. I didn't quite understand but he somehow got caught stocking a creek out in the woods of Yamhill County somewhere with non-native, farm-bred trout so he could fish the river later, and this got him fired. He says it was all a misunderstanding but something in all this didn't add up, yet I didn't want to press it. The first guy he saved was a tweaker who came on site with his family to dump household goods at the Z-wall then wandered off and disappeared, out of his mind. It was pieced together later that he'd broken into a couple houses in the neighborhood across the street, then found his way back, smashed in a window on an outbuilding on site, all the while looking for cash? Clearly delusional, possibly dangerous, Clint caught up with him between yard debris and the landfill, ran him down, tackling him then holding him in a chokehold until cops arrived. I passed the tweaker in my truck sitting on the rear bumper of an ER vehicle looking very pale, wearing eyeliner with long greasy-looking black-dyed hair. Later, Cunningham chided Clint never to pull that shit again because crazies might have a knife. The second instance was a dump truck driver who had been dumping dirt, but something was wrong. Every time I drove by, he was still there, his box in the air. The second time I noticed the truck was in gear, and a drive wheel spun raising up a lot of steam in the mud. The driver was nowhere in sight. I was too busy, I thought, to stop and check it out. Clint passed me so I hollered, alerting him over the radio so he might check it out. Turned out the driver had had a stroke and was slumped behind the wheel over the passenger seat foot still on the throttle. He survived a while before he slipped into a coma later at the hospital. Clint took time out to go visit him at the hospital without knowing he had slipped into a coma. There he found and met the family. He'd known he was sick, they told him, because he'd been sending texts to everyone telling them he loved them. They thanked him deeply for watching out for their Ryan and saving his life.

A minor profundity regarding expediency versus shalom, Andrew

opens the window of the scale and grins at me as he takes the weights log and it's first thing in the morning. He points to something in the window frame that he can see and I don't at first: it's a gorgeous architectural feat of translucent webbing. He shows it to me, ordinary but far from simple, then grabs the stick used for locking the window closed at night and rakes it twice around the three sides rapidly as if playing a triangle. Still grinning—he tears it out—just like that.

Just like candy, Cunningham says, sampling some of his own smoked salmon he brought in and left out on the break room counter for everyone to try. Salmon he caught and cleaned and smoked, then cut into big slabs and laid in a Tupperware. Just to share something good he made with his hands using time and materials from scratch like a grand confectioner. Left with no choice but to text to tell him *Holy shit,* John—that salmon—*so rich so good!!*

typed while standing in the porta-potty urinating just before clocking out on a Wednesday

We are daily witness to the world's wastes

Reading these bad poems of Bly's
I close the book
write some of my own

And just lately, in the last year or so, roll-off trucks bring in 20-yard boxes of dressed, polished stone scrap from kitchen and bathroom countertop installations. This then gets moved and crushed by dozer tracks to make road base for our trucks on soft covered fill. Quarried slabs of imported stone: Italian marble, granite, the boring beautiful grey, or greens and yellows, varieties of white quartzes, green-veined and black dolomites, all scraps leftover from newly built high-end homes.

I talk to myself every time I pass these piles that we are not allowed to salvage, which daily appear and disappear, and ask why this can't be saved--many pieces a half, three quarters or inch thick slabs are three to four feet wide and some strips eight feet long? These might make counters but get junked the company pays to dump. How is this finite resource expensed out on a spreadsheet: too expensive to warehouse, inventory and track, and the cost simply padded and built into each house job the customer pays for? It kills me.

My counters at home are narrow and old covered by 3" X 3" white tile, chipped and cracked black, and the grout a grey turned brownish green with bacteria I can almost see, below cheap veneered cabinets.

Sometimes I walk over to handle the pieces of stone polished on one side only, turning the chunk to see it glint in the sun—catch the surface shimmer and shift, note the complexity of color sparkle in the grain and check the depth for true.

Hobo

On the table a jar appeared one morning, resting, full of legs and eyes and teeth. Without design the Landfill crew and the MRF Ops crew each sit at their own table, just as everyone, when possible, sits in the same seat for lunch or during breaks, without pre-assignment. The old marmalade jar was clear and the glass was wavy because the inside or outside weren't perfectly machined straight, and it had a white, screwed-on lid. For about a week the jar sat at the landfill's table, until during lunch one day Nate moved it over in front of me, saying, "I'm tired of looking at that." I shoved it away from me toward the middle of the table. What was inside was dying of starvation. There were two things in there and they weren't eating each other, though they had plenty of teeth and legs and eyes. It felt like the jar was full of sucking hatred, staring hunger, a magnification of hollow, and maybe violence, or fear, possibly sadness. Their venom and our fear was what got them in there. I didn't want to look at it either. First the big one died—it was a case of mistaken identity, and online I found out this was common, the distinguishing differences being a translucent yellow leg color and the formation of the thorax. The thing we thought it was was actually the thing that preyed on the thing we thought it was, and a good thing to have around for protection against the thing we feared, but Cunningham didn't know this when he stuck them in the jar and brought it, like a grotesque trophy, to sit on the table and starve to death before our eyes every day, while we ate. The glass was lumpy and wavy, but clear. After the first one died (maybe he killed her), the other was left to breathe in the rank smell of the dead one, breathing impossibly stale air, and perhaps air entirely breathed up. Next thing I knew, the jar got moved to the bookshelf under the time clock for another day or two, but he was hanging on to life still, motionless. Eventually both, still in the jar, ended up in the trashcan on their backs, legs folded up. But the strangest thing of all was the reluctance we had to throw the jar away until after what was alive inside had died—then it became okay, finally, for someone, whoever it was. I wanted nothing to do with any of it.

Cat's eye

I unlatched the back door of the trailer and walk back toward the cockpit of the tipper, then to my left and over my shoulder I glimpsed a hulk of shadow lunge toward me from the darkness. Double-taking, I saw nothing there, but the fear was primal and left me with a dull metaphysical unease as if from an invisible blow. I rationalize that perhaps it was a shadow thrown by the packer passing before the light tower, but no that couldn't be it, still, I know better than to write it off as merely the mind playing games with itself. Last night I dreamed I inhabited a floating city and wooden boardwalks radiated from the center like light from the sun. The color of the water was more green than blue but light and opaque and deep, I knew, and the birds in the mangrove trees were colorful and large-beaked. I did not know where I was or why I was there, but it felt like home. Places like this exist on earth, perhaps, but not where I live. I remember and reflect on these fragments orbiting the edges of a spiritual life while walking back toward the cab of the truck to finish settling into the start of a new workday and wait for the creaky electric cleated wheels of dawn.

Vectors

Embrace the suck

–Pat's advice to himself

This safety meeting is on nuisances, referring to noise, dust, and vectors. Vectors are another name for rats, seagulls, cats or any other unintended pests present at every landfill. In Arizona, landfills have Jesus Christ lizards running around like bipeds, while in Hawaii there's a fire they've been unable to put out for fifteen years, and in Alaska vectors are Grizzly bears. Russell, the lead line worker has a scorpion on the back of his neck, tail and stinger poised to strike, visible between his shirt collar and hairline. The black laces on his boots below his cuff are knotted up from breaking and being retied. I see the laces, but not the twisted prior course of events which brought him to this crap job after a long line of many other invisible crap jobs, where he put in time, probably with the same scorpion tattoo on his neck. Russell just had twins, and six kids already before that. He will work his 600 hours here, triggering a background check, in which it will be discovered he is a felon and disqualified from continuing work here, even as a temp, and then he will move on to the next thing.

Drama

He had a pickup and trailer full of household goods which I helped him unload and pitch over the rail into the box on the Z-wall. Because he said he worked for a contractor doing construction, I asked how busy he was staying. Ridiculously busy, he said, so much so we're turning away work. Remodel or housebuilding? We work for investors who buy then flip houses, and right now they're making a killing buying up foreclosures. This one was really sad: they even left their wedding pictures behind.

I emptied the truck bed while he worked on the trailer. I said, It's going to be a really hot day in hell for some of those folks, and out of the corner of my eye I could see him turn and felt his eyes on me. I had a perfectly nice barstool in one hand and a bowling ball in a carrying case in the other, walking, then heaving. He might be wondering whether I blamed him for playing a part in this food chain, so I offered, On the other hand, these people knew they were getting in over their heads, right? No. No, it isn't always their fault, he said. He was throwing laminated kitchen countertops now and was working his way toward broken drywall, and asphalt shingle. I had another barstool, then a cracked mirror, a garden hose and pieces of a treadmill that had been disassembled into manageable parts. The last thing in the truck bed were thick gauge black garbage bags packed full and heavy with what I didn't know. Greed I said, and he agreed. Then I remembered the scale calling a load last week to the MRF as "Teardown from a homeless structure, some tarps, lots of clothing, cardboard." Refuse, discards, remnants, broken bits and pieces and things that no longer work. Luxurious drama of life collected, chewed, worked over, enjoyment broken into suffering material we pay others to pick and push and bury. I worked the Z-wall on Saturdays sometimes. I didn't need to help people unload, and I didn't need to peer into the lives of others. I really don't need to write any of this down. But I do.

Movie

The gull lifts off and flies with the flicker of light and shadow in its wake
                              a ribbon of rainbow colors accompanied by sound and dialog
with tinkly soundtrack music.
                                      Blacks and whites like shadows on the wall thrown,
flickered streams, because he swallowed a reel of videotape
and a length of black ribbon many feet long trails behind
                                                      unreeling
          itself through digestive tract a second at a time.
                                          A glitchy prancing
ten-foot excerpt from *My Little Pony: The Princess Promenade* plays

Deinonychus

I'm unsure how long it took to realize it, but one day I noticed the gulls had stopped flying at the landfill. It wasn't due to lameness though some limped, one-legged, or had empty gouges in their faces where eyes used to be. A few made threatening gestures by lifting their wings high above their backs, arched up like arms, and took on the aspect of fierce angels, hooked beaks like pointed daggers and the avian forward-looking eyes of raptors. Eventually I noticed a molting of feathers, but it wasn't so much molting because they retained the spines or quills of their plumes only losing the soft fletch necessary for flight and lift and the skin underneath took on bizarre hues and color. I was witnessing some sort of metamorphosis but back toward larva or pupae stage rather than butterfly. Maybe in this Oregon landfill I was being transported to prehistoric Liaoning Province to what would become so many millions of years later— (now) —part of the Yixian Formation and that ancient lakebed where even now they are digging up fossils of preflight birds, the Sinosauropteryx. Bird skin without 'feathers' must be ugly, but the gulls were more scaly and reptilian and even the gimpy ones were capable of running more quickly than before—their legs taking on muscle mass, perhaps compensation for being grounded. Still, and unable to leave any longer, mud found a way of reaching up to embrace them as long lost friends, or as if they had always been of earth, dust, grounded, ground. "Sues points out, 'It seems that, genetically, it's not a great trick to make a scale into a filament.'"

Tainted meat and foolishness

I write about you to remember you. And why this is important, I don't know.

My truck is locked-out tagged-out parked in the shop and I'm sitting in the cab staring out the big bay door at a pile of pearlite up on the hill used for solidification and the old cabover Terry used to drive a decade ago, boneyarded now. To my left what catches my eye is an interesting collection of hose clamps stacked and stored from smallest to largest on a display panel made of tall parabolic hoops of metal to designed to hold them. At some point Mark will get off his ass in front of the computer doing POs and shit accounting for his hours on 652798 and actually change out my burst airbag which he estimates an hour to do since he must cage and remove a brake can first. Mark is in big demand right now too—already approached by two roll off drivers while I've been sitting here. I'm most important at least for the moment. He's still not started, however.

I struggle to remember the name of the mechanic who was a meth addict and was kind to me once. I want to say, Bernie, Chuck, Keith? It'll come to me. I'd salvaged some books from the Z-wall. They were a series of digests of great writings of Greeks and Romans and of Western Civ importance from Europe, like Montaigne. The books had been riding in my truck and gotten removed for being in the way of some work. He had thoughtfully set them aside and made sure they weren't tossed, then told me where he'd squirreled them away. Didn't have to do that.

Memorable things about him were his teeth which looked like they'd been eaten away like dissolved brown sugar, in places something grey and bluish. I couldn't imagine how he didn't cut his tongue on that. Also, as a result of bad teeth, he kept cans on the counter of beef consumme for lunch. Other people didn't think highly of him. He was like a wounded animal in the herd that folks felt they needed to distance themselves from out of self-preservation, constantly talking shit about him, his drug habit, etc. What about the yellow iron fleet manager with his giant pockmarked and alcohol bloated nose, Russ? He got a pass, still drinking like a fish, but Kevin—that's it—Kevin! He didn't use anymore, but people assumed he was stupid, incompetent, useless—and mocked him because of his telltale fragments of teeth and what he ate for lunch!

One day I sat down next to him and we talked through our lunch break. Turns out he's been clean for 25 years and had run a recovery center outside of Medford for meth addicts! He said he had lost everything, house, family, worldly belongings. He'd been involved for 10 years or more with that but fearing a relapse hanging out with druggies day in, day out, had had to flee it. Ended up here in this shithole of a shop. Said he was a believer too. Picked up that I was. It was a good talk. Some point later, not too long after this, he stopped showing up to work. I never heard the end of his story, but sometimes at times like now, looking around out here, waiting, I still think of him, his balding thinning, greasy hair, the defective mouth, the thoughtfulness, how long ago all beauty or attraction had fled out of him leaving the shell everyone who looked, saw. I remember and see him as I might the brother you wonder about, but the last thing you'll ever do is look him up. My brother, Kevin. Mark finally gets started, asks me to leave the cab for the break room, so he can finally get after it. As for me, it's finally almost time to go home.

In the break room, before I clock out, Michael says, after I ask, do you remember Kevin, he says who could ever forget Kevin! I ask, "What happened?" "I think he was let go. He could turn a wrench, but he was no mechanic. There was some stuff going on. . .don't get me wrong, he was a nice guy, but. . ." then he continued to blow and wipe his nose.

Getting older
move through days of the week—
starting out Sunday soon enough becomes Friday.

As I was

pulling away at 5:20 AM from the Jack In The Box with my loaded breakfast sandwich and coffee, I first heard the music, then saw her back toward me sitting in her wheelchair at the head of the planter strip divide at the exit to the Sunset Esplanade strip mall, her head moving side to side in a synced rhythm to the music, a kind of unhoused joy, the coming summer morning beautiful, brisk, as sky changes to raw umber. It occurs to me to think about the difficulty of toilets. She mans her post waiting for shoppers to arrive and read her sign, witness her predicament, make their choices to offer alms, give handouts, or simply roll on by only trying to unsee and get on with their lives.

kestrel and meadowlark roosting tree gone—
criss-crossed dozer tracks on the berm—
beauty enough in the patterns, but it's not alive.

Think Green

The company is proud of its waste to energy policies, movement toward cutting edge green and sustainability technologies like plasma burners, etc., and rightly so, is considered the leader in its field. BBQ Bob, the northwest fleet manager, drives a new Ford—a huge extended cab, three-quarter ton, shiny white pickup that never shows any dirt. One decal says WM THINK GREEN, another, opposite, says NASCAR.

Brad, the head operator, rents an old farmhouse on landfill property. In the fenced in front yard are pygmy goats and geese, and out back in the barn he's got pigs, an albino peacock, several dogs and cats, and chickens, turkeys and pheasants that he raises. Inside the house are several kinds of exotic birds: Macaws that he's rescued because they've outlived their owners, an African Grey, and according to him, all his animals run to the door when he gets home, including his pet tortoises. Every day he comes to work with new scratches on his face and arms, which I imagine the pets inflict through affectionate displays, though I've never asked him about these. I recommended he rent a documentary I enjoyed featuring a flock of wild parrots living in downtown San Francisco, which got us talking about his Macaws. He told me that the largest aluminum mine in the world is in Peru, where the Macaws come from and recycling pop cans is important because you could think of each pop can, after mining and production, as roughly equivalent to one Macaw. I understand that no matter what calculus you use, the actual proportion of pop cans to birds must be hyperbolically exaggerated by millions to one—there wouldn't be that many Macaws...

Still, whenever I see a pop can now around the MRF lunchroom or other breakroom trashcans or being used as spittoons which make them nonrecyclable—everywhere but the recycle bins around site—I can't help seeing large colorful parrots become hollow, garish, flightless golems that once held sugary, carbonated liquid.

Randy

As a mechanic Randy was a cowboy. His son, Eddie, was a dumbass—apples and all that. Randy had pulled some strings and gotten him a job as a sorter in a mini excavator, then a few months later he got caught on camera driving doughnuts on the MRF floor in his Jeep like a maniac one morning before work started. So long Eddie. On the wall of the shop office hung an old school metal hardhat with an enormous dent in it, chronicling some epic near miss (or not so near, as the resulting brain damage might account for much). Hung there, I'm guessing, like some *memento mori*, or in his mind, a symbol of his being a badass. Like many here, Randy probably paid his dues in the woods until the logging of timber and mill work fell off.

At the landfill, he started as a heavy equipment operator. Operators and mechanics get paid the same here, so I asked Tim why he switched to working in the shop, his answer was, Because we needed a mechanic, after a pause, and because I think he liked it. From what I could tell the only thing Randy seemed to like about the job was welding. He could be found welding even when far more pressing things needed to be done. The last thing he wanted to do, ever, was work on trucks. Whenever I approached him with a problem he greeted me with, What the fuck do you want! And he was not joking. A lot of mechanics seem to prefer working on yellow iron, as if the only thing that mattered were the dozers, excavators and loaders. They acted put out as though working on trucks was beneath them.

When I got hired, he was the only one in the shop and equipment would enter it, and never leave. Now we have five and it's the same about trucks being the lowest priority. I witnessed him doing an incredibly incompetent job for a couple of years until one day on the grinder he took off half a finger. This still probably wouldn't have gotten him fired, but when the safety man asked him for an explanation, no doubt wishing to be reassured it would never happen again, he said, Shit happens! That did it. Maybe a year later, Debbie placed a card on the table in the breakroom for everybody to sign wishing his widow condolences after his massive coronary. I pulled out a pen, opened the card and wrote, *shit happens*, then signed my name.

"13 acres

backed by Weyerhauser woods and timber, a farmhouse from 1912 in pristine condition.
Everyone wants their piece of land.

It was the wrap-around porches we fell in love with.

And an acre of meadows surrounding the property with a few oaks and elk and deer wandering
up out of the woods that the man living on the property would sit out at dusk to watch.

The Columbia a mere mile away as the crow flies, not too far off the highway outside of
        Clatskanie.
Beautiful streams criss-crossing the property, probably great fishing; an artesian spring
        for drinking water.

The deal fell apart at the end in a bad way.
We had signed documents and paid thousands of dollars for inspections.

The owner was really strange.

It all hinged on mowers and tools and equipment we had brokered into the deal
for an added price after she balked at just throwing it in for the purchase price,

and the man living there—a retired mortician—had some weird relationship to the owner
but she did not live on the property. In his sixties, he revealed she had been his 3rd grade teacher.

At the point where he was supposed to vacate we were told he hadn't left yet.

There was a meeting between all the parties and we were made to understand he
        would not ever be leaving.
At one point in dealing with this crazy woman both brokers broke down, one in anger
        and the other in tears.

But she wouldn't budge.

I assumed at least we'd recover our costs for the money we'd spent—about three grand—
because she had been the one to breach the contract, and that last minute—
but we were forced to eat the cost.

                It's a good thing we didn't get it because Clatskanie
is an hour and a half from here, and we never could have afforded it. Not really.

But I fell in love with that property. We had had to look that far out
because we were on the edge of what we could afford. I'm sure now it would never have
> worked out.

Now of course you know we live in a manufactured home.
Our trailer park in Forest Grove has lots of big old trees.

It's a little cramped now that my ailing father-in-law has moved in with the six of us
but he has his own room where he can crank up the heat."

Pat describes an elk bugling

I've just asked, *What is it about elk?* No,
that was another friend,
Craig, who texted back,
Elk are light and heavy
—buoyant weighty creatures—somehow light on their feet—

More specifically, after showing Pat a Mike McGriff poem,
early on a late October morning before work
while his eyes are still squinched, barely open, he
agreed elk must be poetic, if anything is, and he's not one who traffics in poetry
but humors me and McGriff
and a second later I offer a Dombrowski piece in the same vein
—but even better, I thought—
He acknowledges any attentions to elk might be worthy.

It was then I asked,
not at all sure what I expect him to say,
What does an elk sound like when it bugles?

Immediately voice awake and eyes open,
both holding awe,
— because he has decided to take me there—

Like the head of a god—
it rips through
the underbrush first shaking then tearing
off branches fierce branches coming out of his own head
hide plastered with mud because he's been rolling in it.
Snot running spraying from his nostrils,
rib cage heaving breath in and out
loud with steam
then he tears off a bugle
looking for you—it's wild—not human—
Thirty feet away
All he wants to do is spot you then kill you. . .

*You've pursued this animal three miles
up into a ravine after hearing his bugle
echo from that far away. You are trying to engage
this elk from behind a tree or a stand of trees—
that's really all you have between him and you
—you are this irritation, distraction,
a threat to his herd and his dominance
—and that is everything—
He barely eats while in rut.*

*Suddenly he's thirty feet away
and he rips off a bugle
he's jerking his head through underbrush crashing through branches
eyes rolled up in his head—no fear but anger—
snot spraying out of his nostrils coat covered in mud.
And it's unbelievable!
You tell yourself to calm down to stop the shaking.*

He was sitting in his chair before; now he's standing
and imitates violent trembling.

*His only intention at this moment is to kill you.
He is a beast, screaming—in some way womanly but very
very male too. He's got a cow in estrus and he's all wound up.
Satellite bulls orbit the herd circling,
waiting for their chance and his distraction to move
in on that cow and the herd the bugling bull's protecting,
but all of his attention right now is focused on you.
Your unwelcome presence and challenge.*

You are never quite in your element.

Andrew has walked in, clocks in, hears Pat talking, begins nodding,
adding his bit about half-starved elk too busy to even eat during rut.
Then is when I realize I must be the only male on site
who has never participated in an actual elk hunt.
My interactions with elk have all involved moving vehicles—
trying to miss and *not* to kill them. My mind drifts to the book I'm reading, all

this elk talk bringing to mind a wrinkled brow and a crooked jaw,
the wise ferocity of a white bull sperm whale,
ancient hide shaggy with corroded harpoons
and corkscrewed lances, trailing frayed ropes—
My favorite thing is to pack meat out
—that feeling of accomplishment after—
a difficult hike out—the camaraderie
and the hurt of it, Pat is saying,

and something to Andrew (and me) about bone sour—
when meat gets left on the bone and not cooled off quick enough
so it has this bad taste from the inside out.
First thing you do after cutting it up is find a creek to cool it off
then hang what's left—
whatever you can't place in black trash bags to carry out.

I wish I'd thought to record this, I say.
Pat knows I'll write all of this down.
It's what I do.
He's also aware of my fear of losing just the right words, so he says,
Don't worry about it too much—laughs—
When you're trying to remember how to describe it
Just imagine a powerful creature with trees growing out of its head!

We step out in the morning dark,
part ways heading to our parked, idling trucks,
these mechanical partners not so very different from whales,
little lights aglow and beaming.

Rattus rattus

What's most marvelous about him is how clean and dry he looks. Brown, tan and grey toward the belly, a beautifully complex mixture of streaks of brindled coloring running through the fur—not one, as if some cartoon. I caught movement to my left while I sat in the tractor cab on the tipper while Tim tips, waiting for the trailer to slip down out of the sky to land back with a jolt on my fifth wheel plate and there he was—the last week of rain heavy and he's bouncing along the ridges of mud surrounded by water in the ruts and depressions—navigating wet muddy clods and the several inches of creamy mud patches, moving very quickly, because it's daylight and there's no cover for him so his bounce and scurry is more sprint. He reaches high ground and tufts of undisturbed grass around a gas wellhead. There's perforated orange fencing of inch square holes wrapped around four PVC pipe poles to mark and protect against recklessness what's inside the boundary: gas pipes and valves for the well we've spent all winter building up and burying around. He skirts this fence and disappears from sight: dry, clean, safe for now.

We, so much smarter, the civilized, unwitting stewards, walk around all day mud up to our knee-high muck boots, splatters all over our pants and coats covering us in leaked piss, blood, grease and shit —others' and our own.

Amelia Earhart visits the landfill bearing a gift of wings

"Please know that I am aware of the hazards. I want to do it because I want to do it."

Other than red hair and the name on her credit card, no one would have known her. She wore no airman's cap, no leather bomber jacket. She drove a flatbed in,

loaded with carbon fiber wings. Black and looking like steel, but lighter, tougher.

She had to drive from one end of the landfill to the other without stopping—she said it was just her way. It was also her necessary destination to offload the black wings.

Long and lying strapped to the bed of the trailer, they looked shiny like a beetle's wing covers, but perforated and clearly machined.

Some might want to describe her as aloof but driving long distances across country teaches you certain habits, and to recognize such in others,
which cannot be too dissimilar to crossing an ocean in flight. Similar risks,

the same tedium, the same bargains with time, weather and solitude,
a similar monotony of motor sound and working machinery and air blowing over a hollow body, the same turbulent whistling past a fairing, or grooves in the riveted wing.

The highway is an ocean. Continents are just large islands.
And food and fuel are found only on islands. Islands are moments between transport. At night, clouds and stars and the moon are sliding light. They arc, silent, roiling whitely overhead.

For Amelia the clouds floated sometimes alongside and beneath her. For drivers this occurs only on steeper grades.

One needs a wing or wheels to move something, and to fly or roll. You can't *really* live in the midst of transport—it is too much a kind of work.

She had the look of a cat whose tail won't stop twitching, and an easy, nervous smile.

Of course I wanted to know where she'd been keeping herself lately, but she looked abrupt— feigned lack of comprehension or interest in the discussion, like some famous people will.
Or it might have been hearing loss.

Maybe she suspected I wanted something she didn't have or couldn't give.

She didn't look her age, but younger, and wasn't the least transparent. She seemed to need very little direction, felt comfortable in strange surroundings, neither charging ahead, nor being led by a line.

As I operated the Hitachi unloading her flatbed, I kept sneaking glances at the legendary aviator. Not aviatrix but aviator. She wasn't beautiful, but she was pretty.

If it were up to me I'd have waived the offload fee. I'd have not charged her a dime for this, feeling guilty taking money from such a great American. Surely she'd paid her dues in daring as a woman, a flyer, and to history.

Like so many women, she comes to the dump alone.

Rivets. Heartland.

She rolled up her straps and placed them back in the side kit,
then walked over to me with something in her hand I thought at first was a white stone. Then I realized it was a piece of brain coral.

I asked her what was written on the underside, and she handed it to me and said, "Flying might not be all plain sailing, but the fun of it is worth the price."
I said, "This is what you say to one who drives truck and works in a landfill?"

She headed back to the flatbed, then turned and said, "Yeah—You really oughta get out more."

To detain her just a little more, I called, "I'm dying to know—you and Fred, Nikomaroro?" She reached into a pocket, pulled out and held up her penknife, whispered something I think might have been "...hooey."

She smiled a big toothy brave womany grin, then climbed into the cab of her Peterbilt arm out in a wave as she drove away.

Considering buying a handgun,

I speak with Brad first. What kind and caliber should I be looking for? Strangely, it's as though I've asked a really difficult question when I assumed he would have no problem answering. He's not sure, and his advice is to go to a store and handle them and choose the one that feels most comfortable. He offers to have me over to do some shooting behind the landfill. Terry tells me to get a revolver, because I'm unfamiliar with handguns and less can go wrong. He said steer clear of guns like Glocks that don't have safeties. Get a .38 stainless steel— you can use .357 rounds for more firepower or .38 shells for normal power— they're simple and indestructible and don't require a lot of cleaning. He invites me to meet up with him after work sometime and we can fire a few different firearms, so I can get a feel. Cunningham really thinks I should get a clip gun because that way I can keep it unloaded if I have small children in the house but load it quickly if a home defense issue arises, pull back on the mechanism, and a round is in the chamber in a matter of seconds, compared to a revolver which is harder to load in the dark and half asleep. Terry and Cunningham debate this—Terry says he always has a gun loaded and in the drawer by his bed, whereas Cunningham says he keeps his unloaded and outside his safe but accessible with ammo nearby. Terry thinks clip guns can jam and are more difficult to clean and maintain with more moving parts. They argue about this while I enjoy listening in. At one point they turn to me and ask, don't you have friends who own firearms you can talk to, and I said, yes, but you guys are friends and I'm asking you. Cunningham seems mildly surprised but pleased about this, turns to Terry and says, "He considers us friends." I'm surprised the issue might be in question. It reminds me how we are different—no, I am different, and I probably seem aloof in their eyes, seen to seem, to think myself better, and set apart? The fact, embarrassing to admit, is what I most need right now is a little supplementary training on what it means to be a man.

It's then I realize it would be no less strange, if I were to turn this question around on myself, and one of them asked me, "Who's your favorite poet?" And after stammering a second I'd be forced to say, "It all depends."

Gun nuts

"I just want one," Brad says quietly to himself. Apparently, Clint is a conspiracy theorist, and 2012 and the Mayan calendar came up because it's a couple of weeks before Christmas, so he walked over to the whiteboard and drew a timeline from -3 to 3 stating that the estimate for the apocalypse on December 21st is off by a year, because they don't figure in the zero in the transition from BC to AD. It occurs to me to ask that since the Mayan Empire dated around 300-900 AD how that would be relevant to their calendar, but I don't say anything because I'm still studying the timeline and wondering why having or not having a zero would make the apocalypse happen in 2011 rather than 2012. "Bullshit anyway of course, and an excuse for Hollywood to make a movie," Leo says. They are talking about guns and dwindling freedoms now. I'm remembering something on the radio about a guy in Washougal whose house was on fire and he was shooting an armory of guns and ammunition out the window at the neighborhood as fast as he could shoot. A neighbor reported that you would hear six shots, then fifteen, then six again in the time it took to reload. They found a dead dog shot in the backyard and three burned corpses inside the house: the shooter, and his wife and her twin sister, who were also shot. Brad estimates that Terry has thirty handguns or more, and he has five or six. Terry gets them from a sheriff he knows, who sells them to him at a steep discount, and also somehow funnels free ammunition to him. Good friends I guess or maybe someone he served with in Viet Nam. The police he knows that work in narcotics say if the public knew about the extent and nature of drug trafficking going on in the area, they would never be able to sleep at night, or allow their kids to go outside, even in the backyard during the day. "I just want one," Brad says again, this time looking directly at me. "The day they come for my guns, I don't care who they are, whether they have kids at home, or whether they are in uniform, I just want to take one with me, that's all. After that it won't matter what happens."

Rocky's story

One day I noticed the tattoo beneath his hematite wedding ring, so I asked why some men tattoo a ring on their fingers. He said the reason he did was because he was a welder and couldn't wear one at work and felt it odd not to, and I agreed that made complete sense. Then he took the ring off and showed me the tattoo which displayed a heart handle above a key shape, and said, I'll tell you another story, I call my wife a warden and this is our private joke. And then if you see here, showing me the tattoo on the side of his finger between second and third: 7+3=10. This is the month and day and it just happens to add up to the year we were married. I agreed that was pretty cool and then I asked why he didn't weld anymore. I used to do cosmetic welding and specialty stuff and heavy equipment, but the bottom dropped out in '07. Experienced welders were getting paid 12 bucks an hour when they should have been making 25. That's when I left the trade. Now he drives the sweeper truck on site, and I don't want to know what they pay him.

When asked about tattooed wedding rings, Pat speaks words of welding:

Weld slag...
Mine (wedding ring) is titanium
Steel blued and blacked

Got ten, might as well lose one.
Crushed or cut

ER pictures show
no meat just bone

The metalwork trades

Pain threshold goes up
being burned all the time do a shimmy, flux
overhead welding liquifies
forms a crust that shields from contaminates. Falls.
Light showers from sparks and shield crust
sear. You grow to miss it:
that sting of pain tiny blister
burns from falling fire lit up aimed
bounce off everything
you//concrete//the metal you work.

When I weld in my driveway at home
I wear a wife beater flip flops no gloves just a mask.
Crust pockets
piece of the crust goes in your pockets
goes down your back under your shirt.
Clothing riddled: telltale scorches: burn marks: plenty of frayed holes.

I sit reading

in the jostling truck cab as it's being loaded from the hole above. I am waiting for Claudio, who mans the excavator dumping big bites of trash through the roofless trailer's top from his station playing king of the hill over a pile of residual—both of us call this a job and work. I'm reading a paleontologist's account of his trips to South Africa which span more than a decade of expeditions and field research to investigate the Permian/Triassic extinction which wiped out 95 percent of all life 250 million years ago. His work takes him north of Cape Town to the ancient Karoo, to hunt for fossils of mammal-like reptiles like the Gorgonopsian, built like a bulldog but the size and likeness of a saber tooth tiger. We discover that the extinction is also called the Great Dying and began in the oceans, then proceeded to land. We learn the rocks at the transition point from the green Permian layers turn to red and are laminated, meaning there was no bioturbation, meaning sudden and distinct shift from biota to no biota. There are a range of specialized words geologists use to describe these things. We learn that the rivers changed from meandering to braided, which shouts catastrophe, but the author doesn't allow us to feel stupid for not knowing this. We learn the sadness of the narrator when a brilliant and precocious young student commits suicide after he fails a calculus class, and had he only approached his mentor, this professor, he would have learned that calculus isn't particularly necessary in the field of paleontology— but the student chose instead to die from shame. We learn that when simpler forms die out in these extinctions it makes way for a more diverse variety of forms later. That the Permian mammal-like reptiles gave way to reptiles of the Cretaceous, then after the asteroid strike, reptiles gave way to smaller birds and mammals, but insects survived through it all. We learn that layers of rock and sedimentation which sometimes go on for hundreds of meters represent ages of time and that lower is older and higher is younger. We learn that the extinction was not gradual but also not sudden and occurred after several smaller catastrophic events in a row: continents moved, oceans died of anoxia, volcanic activity in Siberia wiped out plant life, and all this followed by spikes in CO_2 and methane. Oxygen in the atmosphere dropped by more than half, and you can see it locked up in the oxidation of the red rock. Thus, the only survivors were those pre-adapted to high altitudes. We also follow him as he drills for core samples to check for magnetic signature, searches for carbon isotopes, graphs all finds on a stratigraphic chart, and bemoans his lack of fossil-finding acumen compared to his team leaders', and performs many menial tasks. We watch as he muses in a Boer graveyard built next to a stone house in the arid, frigid, fiery Karoo, which rests over a far older graveyard. And I smile in the recognition that many of his day-to-day tasks are tedious in ways similar to mine but makes far less money, and he must occasionally console himself by moving momentarily higher up the sedimentary layers to where the fossils and bones lie on newer beds and outcrops in greater abundance, because the extinction boundary is wearying after looking so long at such absence of life. Dust floats and drifts down around the truck as the trailer is loaded. After closing the covers of the book over the stacks of lines and layering of words on pages which follow one after the other, landfill dust darkening their white edges, I wonder if I might have missed my calling. How might we classify that different kind of death? Claudio hails me over the radio that the load is ready. I throw the book on the seat next to me and almost everything I just read slowly slips from me—the words poured in but must have burst in the air outside my head, because only bits and pieces remain, broken, buried—soon enough all traces forgotten.

Cunningham, spending an idle moment

on a grassy knoll on the backside of the fill, had been scouting for deer with binocs, when he noticed a guy up to his neck in the pond below. When hailed the man did not respond. Only after the police arrived would he answer. He had been in one pond and then moved to another smaller one, walking and swimming. He seemed to think he was on his uncle's property, but in fact the day before he had T-boned a rock with his car, the airbag had deployed, and then after emergency vehicles showed up he managed to slip away unnoticed. But all this was pieced together after the fact from the accident and ensuing missing persons report that occurred 10 miles away in Forest Grove. Apparently he had wandered miles disoriented, possibly with internal hemmorhaging, like someone from a David Lynch movie with multiple identities lurking inside him. He wore tennis shoes with no socks, cargo pants and was shirtless, but bruised from a seatbelt and horribly scratched up from trudging through blackberry brambles to get to the ponds. It's as if, out of a wide landscape, instinctually drawn by some inner magnetism or GPS he sensed this was where the dislocated, damaged and unredeemable belonged, only to find another mysterious, parallel world, containing an unrecognizable family waiting with extended arms on the other side. Also police, fire department, and the ambulance that showed up that day.

Pond

Most summer days in the morning, between trailer loads, I load up the water truck and wet the roads for dust control. Every time the level in the pond drops by some miniscule amount that no one can measure in trips or days, but only after weeks. To properly cover the roads takes two passes and there is enough road area to require four trips to the pond, then Nate wets them similarly in the afternoon. While the truck is loading I have a chance to study the pond. I've seen Canada Geese raise goslings and Mallard's their ducklings, studied a kind of dragonfly that has a black stripe on opaque purplish white wings. Had opportunity to ponder the epochs of ponds and generations over millennia it took to refine their ability to hover and maneuver better than any helicopter, wings shrunk from 3' to 3" spans. I've watched a kingfisher swoop erratically then perch on protruding sticks corner to corner, noticed a beaver trail of mud over the grass from a dragged tail between the smaller, slowly diminishing pond and a larger one nearly a lake to the north. I've watched a blackbird's mouth open and seen the throat move in the branch of a tree a few yards away knowing song was coming out but drowned silent under the pump motor, seen minnows darting in tunnels through waterweed made by a muskrat, heard the feeding clack and squawk of Great Blue herons nesting and feeding in the tops of the nearby pines. All the animals know is loud periodic sound when I appear, silence when I leave and an aftermath of puddles to drink or flap in. They can't connect my appearance with asphyxiation or slow, drying heatdeath any more than an infant or its mother could know that the defective baby formula nursed from the bottle they hold will directly result in a life crippled and spent in a wheelchair after the onset of Multiple Sclerosis. All they know is the abstract sound from an engine working.

Correspondence excerpt regarding Doug, the water truck driver

For Sally

I went to the local Thriftway to get some groceries for dinner and I saw a fellow, the first pass by I didn't recognize him, but walked on by and didn't say anything. Then as I was leaving the store, I caught up to him as he was leaving too, then I recognized him as a person who'd worked at the landfill as a temp about a year ago. His name is Doug and he drove the water truck to wet down the roads when they were dusty and he cleaned tracks on the dozers and yellow iron equipment with the firehose attachment. I would drive the water truck in the morning 5:30 to 8:00, and then hand it off to him once he got to work. He had a paper route to help make ends meet and lived in the Newberg area (the landfill is closer to Portland and 20 miles away) so he and I both had a commute. He would bring me a newspaper and sometimes buy me a Snicker's candy bar just to be nice. It was uncharacteristic generosity. I think he respected the fact that I did a good job before he arrived—I had a routine and was thorough, so it made his job easier. The company is terrible about hiring people and will keep them as temps for years at lower pay and no benefits just because they can. In addition to this they would have him cleaning the tracks on heavy equipment which had come into contact with all manner of chemicals—most of the time we don't even know what the stuff is—seriously, we don't. The company was not fast about getting him protective rain gear since it's the temp agency's responsibility to provide safety gear and the water spray and chemicals were eating through his clothes over time and probably affecting his skin. After a year or a little less he quit. Then after a time I saw him pumping gas briefly at a nearby gas station and he was embarrassed to be seen at this work, I could tell. This is all background.

Anyway, I see him at Naps's and we say hi as we walk out together and we exchanged the usual how you doins. He had a golf putter that he was holding handle down as a cane and was limping and told me his back was hurt. I asked if he was on disability, and he confessed he was still out of work and hadn't found anything. This was an unbelievably common situation, especially at the landfill, or in past jobs I've had which are hard physically, like truck driving, delivering Dollar Tree store freight in which the personnel there have lives which literally unravel before a co-worker's eyes. It's something I'm used to in other words, usually revolving around a marriage breakup, physical injury or degeneration which prevents one from continuing to make a livelihood, or joblessness, bankruptcy, addiction to substances, all of which can destabilize your life, etc., or any combination of these. All this to say that I'm not surprised or particularly paying attention to this—not that I'm without empathy for the details but it's not shocking news and pervasive contact with personal tragedy in others often enough and you can get desensitized to individual acquaintances if you let yourself lose an *imago dei* perspective. On the other hand, if you pay too much attention without the proper perspective it can get to be too much too fast. I suspect there is a kind of career, of the white-collar kind, in which this never becomes an issue? Tragedy is always a second away for each of us, but folks in this other context seem to walk a few inches above the ground and not to live their lives so close and in such violent proximity with the various manifestations of it on a daily basis, and can more easily kid themselves about their security, insulated by means, stability, abilities and material blessings as they must be. For Doug, I saw now joblessness, physical disability and probably a family life that's a disaster in the background, and impending homelessness in the future, with zero 'safety net'—this was between the lines that I understood below everything, while on the surface he was this acquaintance I had bumped into at the market whom I was spending a minute with, before I got on with the rest of my life. At bottom, everyone has some story like this—either in the past or the future—it's pervasive.

He said he had a job opportunity in Sheridan, a town 50 miles away, and was going to stay with friends while he was there applying for it. I'm thinking to myself that he's looking crippled, approaching fifty, what are the odds of this working out? I said that sounds really hard, how are you holding up without work or money and disabled, and he said without the grace of God I don't know where I'd be—honestly, it's the only thing keeping me going. I told him I'd pray for him as I remembered and thought of him. His face lit up as he realized we were both Christians. Then, wanting to offer some wisdom, or support or something just right to encourage, I proceeded to mouth what sounded to me to be short, empty platitudes like, well, hope it all works out, and hang in there, etc., my desire was to try to communicate something worthwhile but confronting how it all looked on the face of it, I was left only with inarticulate filler phrases, and I believe he somehow saw through to my underlying skepticism. At this point we said our goodbyes, and he got a kind of a hard look on his face as he passed in front of me and limped away. I realized too late that it was to the bus stop and not a car. If not for the awkwardness I might have offered to give him a ride somewhere, but I just drove home with my groceries. I sensed this had been a divine appointment and my job was to pray for him and encourage him. To me it seemed like perhaps the only reason we met in that store was so God might say to him, "I see what you're going through and I'm aware of all the details and you aren't alone in this. I am with you. Even while your circumstances are dire." A person faced with this knowledge can always go one of two ways: Take comfort, or get really pissed off. I hoped that Doug was the former type.

What was remarkable about this were the next two things that happened. What I've just described is not something totally unusual, right? When I got home, I made dinner and Sally and I sat down in front of the TV to eat it, and at some point I told her the story I just told you, except in the middle of it I broke down, sobbing uncontrollably and completely unexpectedly. I could imagine Doug causing some of this stuff by his own choices, but everything I'd seen of him suggested he was doing the best he could to be responsible and hold things together but despite this, shit just kept happening, and it caused me to wonder why Christians experience such hard providences. I suspected that this was the Holy Spirit giving me a gift of empathic love—I've had this happen only a couple times before. It's so unexpected, sudden, and so strong a feeling that it's clear it's supernatural. So, I decided, and Sally agreed, it was a sign I should really be praying for this guy. I said in frustration to her, How—what do I pray? She said, you know, the obvious stuff—for healing and a job…hard for me to believe it could be that simple.

Fast forward several weeks. Cunningham, my foreman, walked up to me as I was heading out to lunch. The Cottage usually makes me a lunch, but this day they didn't. So, I was having to go out for lunch and Cunningham said, where you going, and can I come along? This has never happened before. On the way to the fast-food place, he gets a call, looks at the ID and says, "Yuck." He answers and says, Hello, Doug—who proceeds to tell him he got a job in Sheridan. I asked him after the call, Is this the Doug who used to drive the water truck? He went on to tell me that Doug used to work for Stimson mill, the same place Cunningham had been foreman before taking this job, and that Doug did a highly skilled job there for about 6 years before that part of the mill had gone out of business—that's how he'd known him. I had just prayed for Doug that morning and was wondering how he was doing and if I should keep praying for him and how. I wasn't remembering everyday but every so often. The upshot was that God used both Doug in my life and me in Doug's to say, "I'm there, watching and working, in the midst of your daily mundane and sometimes awful details and circumstances and I can and do orchestrate the tiniest circumstances. Don't you doubt it…"

It was extremely encouraging. I actually now think I was the pathetic one most in need of healing and lacking in faith, not Doug at all. He had no use for my pity, and I'm not even sure he or God needed my prayer. My prayer for him, I think, turned out to be more for myself—to transform me!

Travis 2, Temp mechanic

On the inside running the length of his left forearm in Greek characters was "Jesus wept." Because he's a mechanic, and they all wear orange jumpsuits, I feel like I'm sitting across from an inmate; he pulls his little red kid's lunchbox out—this is new. He used to bring it in a black plastic trash bag he would reuse—maybe the lunchbox is something he fished from the line pile. He explains the context of 'Jesus wept,' and knows it has to do with Jesus' 'buddy,' Lazarus—mentions Leviticus and the prohibition against marking one's body. He wanted the tattoo to be prominent, but discreet, a reminder and *memento mori* with a twist. "I haven't talked to Him for a long time. Too long. I'm the son of gypsy biker hippies and grew up on a commune." Bald, tall, and thin with sharp features, always speaking fast and very intelligently; there's something cunning or off-putting about his mere appearance, but now, past that, I want to know more.

One day he abruptly said goodbye to all in the lunchroom but in his haste to leave he'd forgotten his little red lunchbox and had to come back for it. "What happened?" I asked for the room. "I was fired for using tools unsafely—they're right, after all these years, what do I know?" he explained. Then he was gone.

Four

Bliss — a-second-by-second joy and gratitude at the gift of being alive, conscious — lies on the other side of crushing, crushing boredom. Pay close attention to the most tedious thing you can find (Tax Returns, Televised Golf) and, in waves, a boredom like you've never known will wash over you and just about kill you. Ride these out, and it's like stepping from black and white into color. Like water after days in the desert. Instant bliss in every atom.

–David Foster Wallace, from a typed note found with the manuscript of *The Pale King*

...from the dust and ashes of forgotten centuries, the secrets of a life extinct for the general eye, but still glowing in the embers...What else than a natural and mighty palimpsest is the human brain?...Everlasting ideas, images, feelings have fallen upon your brain softly as light. Each succession has seemed to bury all that went before. And yet, in reality, not one has been extinguished.

–De Quincey, from the essay "The Rose of Paracelsus"

'My memory, Sir, is like a garbage heap.'

–Jorge Luis Borges, from "Funes, His Memory" in *Artifices*

Every brushed shoulder, handshake, kiss leaves millions of skins cells. People assume we're all discrete and contained individuals, but lab techs know that life is effluvia.

–Diana Abu-Jaber, from *Origin*

The one God loves

for Dave Graham

Chris wanted to do something to help out the line guys. Instead of turkeys this year for Thanksgiving he researched the cost of hams because they're pre-cooked, knowing some guys might not have ovens or the knowhow for cooking a giant bird. He explained all this during the safety debrief meeting after a roll-off driver got crushed against his truck by the backing loader on the tipping floor in St. Paul, MN. One wasn't looking—the other trusted too much. After most company-related deaths we have to meet to talk about it, which is at least once a year.

The hams were very expensive, but he discovered that Honey Baked Ham also offered affordable cooked turkeys for sale, and there was a choice between smoked or Cajun-style.

Finally, November rolled around. In the conference room of the admin building, fifty cases of frozen, cooked turkeys were stacked up against the wall. It was Friday and we all finished early. I sat in the cab, parked, filling out my DVIR, my turkey resting on the catwalk behind the cab of the tractor, driver door cocked open,

while line guys filed out of the MRF, walking en masse toward the admin building past where I was parked to get their turkeys before heading back to their transportation by the MRF, then home. Many of them had their neck gators pulled up—COVID. The bulk of them walked in and a few minutes later walked out carrying their cases.

A second group of stragglers was coming over from the MRF, and one walked in stumbling steps. He could only take a half step with one leg and shuffle the other forward stumble tripping like a prisoner in shackles, but it was clear his whole body was afflicted with some disabling condition. It was astonishing to me that he could or would work on the line.

Someone who had the look of a foreman in the returning group rushed over to him and offered up his turkey, handing it off to save him having to hobble any further than he had to, then crossed back again to the admin building to get another for himself.

I watched how the crippled man held the turkey in his right hand then turned and started his trek back to the MRF, this time with the added 20-pound burden swinging at his side. He was struggling but determined. I watched him for a while marveling that he worked despite this significant impairment.

I thought about home for him (group home, tent?) and his living conditions including family context, if he had one. I tried to put myself in his shoes. I thought about the triumph of holding a box with frozen cooked meat and the idea of a holiday that precipitated a gift like this from a boss surrounding a day for the purpose of giving thanks for your lot, your life, your living in a free country, and at peace. Or maybe instead slowly and completely getting drunk off your ass on a case of PBR?

I realized that whatever scenario I would imagine for this man might possibly approach the reality and difficulty perhaps, but could never be perfectly accurate: his story, whatever it was, had brought him here to this time and place. He had ended up in this shit job, and did it. Nobody gets a pass on suffering but some get such nice big helpings. And why would I insult him by making shit up?

I considered the thoughtfulness of Chris who didn't become a regional site manager overnight, but started out in the shop as a mechanic and had tattooed sleeves and a gutter mouth to prove it. Worked his way up. He likes to say they gave him this cake job at the most lucrative site in the country to reward him. So he could kick back. He came up from Texas driving his Mustang muscle car.

I thought about getting out of my truck and going to help this guy to wherever he was going with that damn turkey. All the rest walking by him, not attempting to help or ease his burden, all having moved on. But then I considered the dignity of people with disabilities who don't always want or need help and the wrong committed if they prefer to manage on their own. I thought about the nurse who told me if you worked in a senior center, the memory care unit, and if a patient can still button their own shirt, they damn well should be allowed to do it, like any other image bearer.

So, I sat and watched from my truck, at my far remove, as he half-stepped, shaky, each step looking as if it cost him dearly, but he continued on, carrying that feast in his hand. His halting, faltering step had the look of one walking on the balls of their joints moving in ground glass instead of cartilage. Then I removed my phone and took a fucking picture.

I wanted to remember this.

The man who was a foreman, I'm guessing, who probably knew this man by name, and perhaps some of his circumstances, maybe even all the sordid, mysteriously determined details of his luminous life, had already retrieved his second turkey and recrossed the ground back to him in the time it took for the crippled man to make it to the corner of the MRF, where finally he passed beyond my line of sight.

There were about 18 line guys though the number varied as many failed to show up on a given day—and this one man, messed up as he was physically was working rather than living or dying on the street. This amazed me, that he had a job paying so very little, and a hard one,

that he may not be doing all that well, but somehow he showed up, did it, and took home his turkey which he earned, despite it being a gift, because now he must carry it home to whoever might be waiting there for it, or perhaps just himself. Assuming he wasn't living out of a Conex box on site. . .

Surely here is a man God loves. See him glow in a halo of pain and want he must stand in. Walk in.

Only one thing I wish. I wish I at least knew his name—a name to go with the picture. God's love has made him holy. I just want something of his I might take to keep.

Night owl

Andrew says he's a night owl. This gets Pat talking. He always stumbles into the break room with his eyes closed, heads straight for the coffee Jack made. Later he tells me he makes himself go to bed at 8:30. Back when he was a welder repairing damaged drop boxes and commuting to Portland, how he was being written up for showing up late all the time and close to losing his job. His life was out of control, and he just couldn't be disciplined enough to go to bed early. He would get up at 2:30 in the morning knowing it would take him an hour to prepare his lunch because he couldn't even open his eyes. He flails his arms like a sleepwalker to demonstrate. He was waking up while leaving the road. Like being a drunk driver, I said. Yeah, he said, Exactly—it was horrible. He said one morning he was coming in from Mollala and when he got to Oregon City was driving through town, fell asleep, then woke up after hitting someone walking through a crosswalk. He stopped to get out and look, positive he'd killed someone. Blood and hair all over the bumper but discovered it had been a deer. A deer crossing the street using the crosswalk. He was so relieved but shaken by this that he straightened himself out—no more falling asleep and getting to work late. Now it's 8:30 sharp every night, going to bed not much later than his kids.

And the Lord said,

I need someone to do this job for me:
Not the best job
it isn't filled with greatness
meaning or purpose, but lowly—
Still, someone has to do it
and I think you'd be perfect for it.
Will you do it?

Also, someone needs to pull this crappy trailer
full of holes that pulls crooked and dog tracks badly
to the right—
Either you or my other son, Pat—
how about if we spare him that—Will you do it?
I know it'll be a minor pain in the ass
and it's slightly less than heroic,
but it's you or him. I want you to remember
a couple summer's back how he offered to trade trucks with you in August
when his AC was working and yours wasn't?
How 'bout you take it on, instead of him?

So I said, *Yes, sure, Lord.* To both things.
And the Lord was glad because I took those things,
high as I am, and he did not need to go ask another
more lowly who might say no or might say yes.
Why not me? What else have I got to do more pressing
than to answer a call when and if it comes?
Now, every day, I must remind myself.

Nothing personal

The senselessness of the alarm sounding, *beep beep* pause *beep beep*, somewhere in the woodpile in yard debris. I heard it after I drove in and started unlocking doors and clocked in. Then I heard it displaced in the darkness, over there somewhere, as I fired up the light tower. It continues to sound, which was its purpose, even after its purpose is no longer needed or wanted, even after being discarded, because it was made to do this and because of a battery and maybe a piece of wood pressing inadvertently on a button. There is nothing stubborn or emotional about this, or even willful—just a mechanical fulfillment of a sequence of actions carried out through design and circumstance to serve animate, conscious persons. But still, considering all this in the dark, after the diesel motor of the light tower has been primed by turning the key backward, then started, but before the lamps illuminate—they are slow to illuminate—questions arise: If it was functional, why had it been discarded? If it was a good little alarm, having perfect faith in its Creator, and doing just what it was told, and continuing to do so even after being consigned to a junked woodpile, never complaining while waiting for the dawn, for that moment when it will eventually be grabbed by an excavator bucket and thumb in a bite with two by fours, pallets, or chunks of broken furniture perhaps or branches and tossed into the grinder and turned into hogfuel—still faithfully beep beeping in the dark of night and beyond—how could it come to this? Whose unjust judgment? This end, this disavowal, this lonely waiting in the outer darkness of a trash heap? There is no meaning to this, we raise up and we tear down, because we can. Nothing personal. But don't fear, little alarm, I whisper, *It will soon be over for you.*

Bizet

Next to the tipper, amongst the rubble, is a shard of a vinyl record I unwittingly step on and catch fragments of a ghostly sound, something like singing that sounds like buzzing or violins and woodwinds tuning, broken arias played backwards, a scritching. Maybe an orchestra warming up before *Carmen*. On the label I can make out bzzz bzzz bizayy but not enough of the label survives to make out the works contained in the grooves. The shard is shaped like a knife, a key without a lock to insert it, then the sound gets cut short like his life. Son Jacques went to school with Marcel Proust and his wife Genevieve was featured as the Duchess de Guermantes and Odette de Crecy in his *À la recherche du temps perdu*. And inside every fig, a dead wasp.

Protocluster

All the way out to the edge of the observable universe crammed
into space a mere 3 X the size of our galaxy are 14 starburst galaxies
on an inevitable collision course about to translate into some colossal
galaxy cluster so God-trashed, and not only the most massive, but also proving to be
the most active area of the known universe
—all this thisness!—they manifest simply as light, but still reach us
from something like 12.4 billion years ago, or, not that long
after the inception of the universe.
                      Such galaxies contain literally 10,000 supernovae going off
simultaneously. Starburst galaxies form stars at a furious pace
making new stars, for comparison, a 1,000 X faster than star-formation in the Milky Way.
Might this not be a good thing—to
                      work so fast,
                      so efficient—
                      so much in so
                      tiny a space?!

Astrophysicists are
            scratching their heads,

        saying,
                We don't know how this is possible—
nothing that big and that active should have been able to form so long ago!
We see the structure of the universe building up slowly from little bits,
and then merging to make bigger bits. We don't expect bigger galaxies
to form until until much later.   Reading about all this at the dump
in the breakroom
                I picture dozers struggling to push trash uphill,
muddy uneven crooked commercial pads too small—
        traffic flow working at cross purposes—
lines of trucks backed up all the way to the wheelwash a mile away,
I conceive of less spectacular
                    clusters in my cute little corner of the Milky Way,
suddenly so
ecstatic for this brand new perspective puzzling eggheads so like
landfill engineers, so fallible, so full of their abilities in their own eyes,
to plan
      and *know shit*.
Meanwhile, the stars and galaxies do what they do not answerable
        while we haul and bury mountains
of other people's refuse, day in, day out, forming our constellations in spaces
too small, tiny little answerable miracles on our own particle horizon.

Sonny

Keep calm   live aloha

—stickered letters on the brim of his hardhat

Poor, morose Sonny with his puffy middle-aged and melancholic Hawaiian face looks my way as I'm passing before climbing into the excavator resting on the concrete pad. He appears smudged pasty and stooped like someone rubbed all the color out of him; all hardness and definition of outline smeared away. We all live boring lives, some of us more hopeless about it than the rest. Routine and the senseless grinding away gets him down, and he confides in me at the tipper, *Don't know how much longer I can do this. I just don't know how much longer.* Then a month later in the dozer, enacting another stupid day following the next inane plan, with a wry grin he holds index finger to temple and pulls the thumb trigger, tiny headjerk from the blast. What else can I do but laugh, shake my head, shrug? Months later, *There is no plan, Dave,* he says. I don't know what to say to this statement of the obvious except to nod my agreement. The sticker letters he put on his hard hat are wearing away. I've tattooed my wrists in a similar vein with a visual invocation I use to remind myself who I am and to whom I belong. His is less permanent but he keeps showing up for another day and another and another. Finally, he escaped our gulag, getting a job at Knife River. Worked his last two weeks and then returned no more, like some others I have loved—this makes me so unbelievably happy.

Update from Dustin:

Text to Clint #1

Good morning! U guys doing anything fun for Memorial Day weekend? I watched Top Gun 2 last night and it was as good or better than the original 🛩️ 👍 👍 I got my first job washing dishes at a pizza place in 1986 at age 14 two months after I saw the original Top Gun to start saving money for flying lessons. I officially retired on my 50th birthday in April of this year and 36 years later celebrated by watching the sequel. My entire work life fell between the two movies 😆 hope u guys are doing well 😎

Text #2

I sold my renegade and will be traveling and living out of a back pack for the foreseeable future 🎒 I'm in prineville now to take advantage of the drier weather and will be back at the coast from the 4th of July through September. My dad bought a place in Yuma Arizona and we will snow bird there for 6 months from thanksgiving to the end of April. Here's a pic of my pack and bug net ⛺

Leo

For a long time, and a long time ago, before Bill, before Lieutenant Dan, Leo was the westside loader operator and he was good at it. Although he was actually of Inuit descent, he looked vaguely Hispanic, so customers were always trying to talk to him in Spanish, which annoyed hell out of him and he refused to speak it even though his wife was from a large Mexican family. Like so many others here he had suffered a broken marriage, though Leo remained married, with wife and kids living in LA, and he went down to visit them a couple times each year. She had chosen living with family and LA over him, or at least this is how he told it. When he chose to leave LA she wouldn't go with him so now he rented a houseboat in Scappoose, moored on the Columbia, and shared it with his mother.

After a brief but serious illness that we never really did get the details on, Leo quit smoking. This surprised all of us, because his daily routine after work every night was to go to one bar in Gaston, the One Horse, and then end at the Diamond Palace Bar in Forest Grove till closing time, and it's hard not to smoke in an environment like that. He said he goes outside to stand with them while they light up. Then, after a year or less he started up again. And I want to say that this *can* comprise a life. Some time and a little while later he just never showed up for work one day. We never were told why. Because sometimes you just don't get to hear the end of the story.

Mark

had a building contractor business and a million-dollar home, then his wife cheated on him and sued for a divorce and he lost the house because, while living in it, she chose not to make mortgage payments for almost a year. After the economic downturn one day he just stopped getting calls for work and his business dried up seemingly overnight. He and his wife fight over the four kids as is usually the case—occasionally it gets ugly and cops are called but he is saved by recordings he makes furtively on his phone. He has tremors which look to me to be the beginnings of Parkinson's though he refuses to call it by that name to me even though he takes serious drugs for the condition which causes him to nod off all the time at work. Now he has been reduced to working as a temp for the landfill making 14 bucks an hour. For some people a life crumbles before your eyes and you must ask yourself what the fuck they might have done to warrant these circumstances. Mark is solid. Decent! He comes over for some extra cash to help me remodel my bathrooms and as he listens to me cuss, tells me my tattoos are burning, which gives me the opportunity to explain the counter-intuitive secret of how really to escape the fiery judgment of Hell.

I wanted to interrupt

In the cab of the tractor, I looked up from my book, and for a brief moment I caught a glimpse of David Foster Wallace striding down the tunnel ramp toward the truck. He wore a bandanna but no hardhat. There, then nearly as fast gone, so I went back to my reading of a conversation between him and Lipsky. Poor kind of stupid Lipsky. Indirectly I was involved—an eavesdropper—as if in the backseat listening in, but unable to interrupt, like a ghost. God, invisibly there too, then and now—not choosing to interrupt. I think now about driving a cabover south from Chicago down 57 through Illinois around that time in '96 through such a hard driving rain the wipers left a sheet of blur in each wake the length of the state. *Son of a bitch!*

the meaning of the windshield in the previous poem

The blurry windshield is a veil—between life and death, between the past and the present, and between human beings who run in circles around each other in time and places, meet through writing and reading, but never meet in life. Some talent or artifact that is produced can artificially blow a person up through glory or notoriety elevating them to a status of near divinity. One forgets their humanity and ordinariness until we hear of some slip or failure or their death, but even then they may live on through the historical record, music, books or films they leave us behind. Fame and the varying degrees of it is a funny thing—it brings you to the attention of strangers, and strangers may feel they know you without your awareness they exist.

At one point in the book (*Although*) a fan comes up to Wallace at a signing and tries to establish a moment of intimacy without knowing it isn't the time and place. Wallace and Lipsky recognize this and talk about it in the car later—the two-way thing isn't possible.

And yet there are connections and we all interact and are connected, if only it's to write and another to read. I think my complaint is over the ephemerality and change and transience. Or the illusion of such. That's what the windshield's about.

Glory can't save you. It is a false friend—a dangerous friend, fickle and short-lived, as it operates in this present world, and it is only a stand-in for something authentic later that we only glimpse in counterfeit now because what we take as originating in ourselves was actually intended to reflect another after operating through us as given and used then transformed into something unique. So—glory is in the new combination of something offered, pointing back at the giver, plus us becoming wholly new and other.

We are designed for applause: to give it and receive it.

Wallace longed for love, and connection. Even he admitted somewhere that's why he wrote *Infinite Jest*. What we long for is to know and be known, to see and be seen, and a book can be a kind of bridge. But not really. That's what's heartbreaking.

Owl in a box

Both Mary and Martha say to Jesus who stalled an extra two days to further magnify God's glory—, "Lord, if only you'd been here Lazarus would not have died."

The next day I saw another owlet, huddled like a mound of mildew in a concavity of concrete, a flaw in the pour, and barely outside the foot-wide wheel rut, its head scrunched down looking asleep. I headed over to the shop and grabbed a box in order to protect this owl and prevent what happened the day before to its sibling, runover with a broken neck. I figured I could keep this one out of harm's way, collect him at the end of the day then drive him to an Audubon Society rep nearby. I picked him up without any response or movement suggesting he even woke up, then set him in the box and closed the flaps, interleaving them closed, and placed it out of direct sunlight up on the shelf next to the exit ramp. I kept an eye on the box to see if it was jostling around and purposely avoided looking to check in on the owlet for fear of disturbing or startling the bird to any greater degree of distress. The box never appeared to move, and holes cut for handles let in plenty of light so the box was not blacked out inside. At the end of the day, after about eight hours, I opened the box finally to discover the owlet laying on its side, head in the corner, wing partially stretched like a shield, eyes half-closed underneath, contorted right leg and talon, perfectly stiff and still. It was a confined space. There was room to stand up but not stretch its wings and perhaps it grew so stressed due from fright and hyperventilated, or perhaps dying of dehydration? I was shocked at the fragility and the notion it could die working itself into a frenzy of terror— just die of that? There was a smudged stain of black and white panic on the bottom of the box. It must have been dead for several hours to become this stiff.

How much longer
   must I continue blindly
my job in this dark
   cardboard box
in the best and safest place
   ,impatiently,
waiting till the end
   of a long long shift?
Is this how *I*
   am to serve you, Lord?

Not empty

After more than a decade of hauling trash uphill I knew how wasteful it was to come back down to the tunnel empty. Dead-heading in long-haul trucking is avoided. It's neither economical nor is it green. Thinking more about it, I realized after each tip I had actually been bringing a backhaul down the hill. An exchange always takes place. Replacing the residual falling out through the swinging back door was color and light. A swirl of hurricane and unquiet seas slipping in behind to backfill the sliding void. Things visible and invisible entered the trailer like information, or for example, the prayers of the people. And if a quantum multitude of angels could fit on the head of a pin I knew it was beyond my imagination to comprehend a number this possum-belly trailer might hold. Time was there with butterflies and all the movies Hollywood could generate on dead videotape flapping from a mirror or snagged on a tarp-securing bracket. Dreams had been conceived to be birthed later. Truck exhaust from the stack billows behind and clouds of highlighted text with awe and deformity and rain fallen from the sky splattered into pieces to rejoin in pools later, jarred and bouncing along, with sounds. The grotesquerie of empty yet not empty sublime because the trailer has no roof to keep elements out and at night starlight enters. The universe was there, trip after trip—it was all there.

illuminated

The barn owl opened its beak. Inside I saw the gulf oil spill and a Precambrian expanse gushing out hundreds of thousands of gallons per minute. Somehow, without sophisticated equipment or heavy calculus, I intuitively discerned the flow rate of the dead, and like an event horizon I could see the past and future rushing toward each other and falling toward me simultaneously, without crashing, without even touching. Then the owl gagged twice and a small slick pellet dropped to the concrete full of bones but all neatly wrapped up in glistening fur. Before it flew the mouth opened again and what came out this time, only sound. Black forests welled up, echoing, to touch sky again. Then the bird shone, dimming the surrounding stars, gathering in murk to fall on sound-damped feathers—saying, *Fear not*.

Death of bowling and the various use of heads

Some objects become something other, a new thing, when jarred out of context and separated from the purpose for which they were created. On the MRF tipping floor a bowling ball becomes a thing of sadness and fear. They arrive on Goodwill loads.

Sadness, because their arrival in such large numbers signals the death of a sport, a previous generation's pastime, some end of an era—now these men or their children sit in front of a flatscreen watching the movement of light and images representing other people's activity, drugged by illusions and opioids, alone, sedentary.

Fear, because those hard polyurethane cannonballs can shoot toward someone lethally when wedged between a loader or backing truck tire and the floor. And once, after the MRF first opened, an operator named Tim picked up a ball between the bucket and thumb of his excavator and pinched it at the operator on the other side of the building as if they could play catch—it rocketed over toward Robert, bounced off a wall, punching a hole in the sheeting, and dropped down on his machine's counterweight, denting the cab deck as if hit by a giant piece of hail. Any machine that must grapple with them is at risk and like marbles under bare feet they roll everywhere.

Another issue is the dolls' heads which invariably come apart from the body. They litter the landing which is a wide plateau at the top of the cell that houses the tipper and special waste commercial dumping grounds. You might think it would be easy to view them as merely hollow plastic, just the remnant of some toy, not real flesh and blood, not a decapitated baby or toddler. Still, it can be disturbing, despite running through this calming rationale, whether because it's an infant's head and how we're wired, or because they're designed to look so very lifelike has never been clear and isn't the point. The point is it requires work to see them for what they are rather than what they seem. The heads get mixed by the sorter in with the small chunks of concrete used for road base, and after rains they float to the top, so that on an early, dark morning it's not a stretch to see an icy plain covered in complaining human faces that must be stepped on to pass through. Here they lie, dusty, muddy, skulls cracked open, faces dented by tires, the delicate features of nursing newborns peaceful, or smiling, eyes lidded at rest, or staring open amidst the glitter of broken glass. I've never heard an infant's cry but the silence and crunching tires is discordant also.

Somewhere I've read due to the quirks of physics and anatomy the heads of suicide bombers remain intact and become a grisly projectile calculated to add to the horror of their last act.

Sleeping Dragonfly

The dragonfly slept dreaming in the door handle of my roll-off truck and in the cool morning was unable to fly.

How many times have I pulled into a truckstop, dropped hypnagogic into the sleeper, shoes barely kicked off

and lied there like that resting before welcome sleep should fall, awaiting new sunlight to warm the cab?

Merton's teasels.

Just beyond the mud grates across the gravel road from the broken-up concrete brought here little load after little load and sprouting twisted rebar that holds its own busted beauty—sidewalk, road, building—useful once, now barbaric, apocalyptic—there is a stand of teasels that I want to draw slowly, sparingly, lovingly with pencil, but know I never will. I lack the skill to capture them. The stalks are long and narrow spiked with tiny thorns. Their heads dampened with rain have darkened and show off even more the ovoid symmetry of the barb-like points, their perfect spines protruding from geometric hollows where seeds were, and below these droops longer ones, wild and erratic like petals twisted, some raised like arms. Evenly spaced; an audience of the dead they still stand, taut and silent. As the grass greens new ones will spring up displacing the old—catch me unawares— then ring themselves with lavender. They remind me of Merton's teasels from the cover of his book but far more beautiful. His black and white photo strikes me as haphazard—blurrily austere. You will barely notice once the living replaces the dead then blooms.

Rejoice, O Florence, since you are so great

Remember this: no matter how dirty your hands are, they're clean enough for another chew.

— Clint Miller

The girls in the scale house change their masks, color to color, style to style, faster than fingernail polish, and this morning not even nine o'clock, Jen has already changed out of a hi-vis to a black one with a horizontal strip of reflective tape sewn across the mouth. I comment on this and she says, I want to wear the hi-vis, but it's too tight.

We share a grin about masks as accessory and coping, she bent over to be heard through the pass-through below temporary plexiglass, to speak to me, who remains maskless in my truck. During the pause while I think what to say her eyes betray a huge grin invisible behind the cloth. At last I shout from the cab, Well, it's all about fashion!

Meanwhile, the country deconstructs, and heals, finally—finally able to shut up about and ignore again its stupid and ugly half; while I trudge through the *Commedia*, laboriously, canto by canto, line by line, footnote by footnote. Just now our two led by ten demons on a fool's errand, noting sinners, who, like frogs on a bank, dive under boiling pitch to escape the approach of the demons' flaying forks and hooks.

And meadowlarks gather to go apeshit in the fields again,
fly fast before my accelerating truck—first flowers yet to appear—
but spring, that mustard fever, is turning on.

Covered

Dave's wall at home probably looks like my trophy wall with book-lined shelves where he can look upon everything he's conquered.

— Pat Sargent

The safety meeting was on alcohol and drug use, and the consequences for coming into work intoxicated, and at what blood levels. We talked about brands of whiskey we liked best, and how Ragsdale prefers rum and is beginning an affair with Bacardi, and the way he says the word, it sounds like he's cheating on his wife. How Terry has a line on 100-year-old Pendleton found in an abandoned warehouse out toward the Dalles. We discussed the byproduct of marijuana growers being dumped at the Z-wall and Alan's uncanny nose for this. After the cops had been called and showed up, they said don't bother us, it's stems and leavings, just treat it like any other yard debris. Returning Iraq vets means exponential medical marijuana hikes, and corresponding waste. Would the temps working the line set it aside and try to smoke it? There was unanimous agreement. Terry brought up his worry about secondhand smoke while visiting a friend's house where joints are always being lit. And what substances a drug test checks for and how much might trigger a fail. We discussed who came up for a random recently, and what the protocol is when that happens. What happens if you refuse, which has been determined to be admitting guilt and makes you subject to termination. We discussed salmon and steelhead fishing and how Cunningham, rather than shine off the tarnish because he always buys new ones anyway, gave his old spinners and wobblers to Raul, who does load inspections at the front gate, and how excited Raul was to get a couple tackleboxes worth of lures as hand-me-downs. We discussed the introduction of wolves into eastern Oregon, and the two-hundred-and-thirty-pound wolf Tim's friend shot in Alberta and posed holding it up for the photo and the thing looked bigger than he was. We discussed the chill of hearing wolves howl from one summit to another when you're standing in the valley at Cunningham's in-law's ranch in Montana, but how stupid it is to reintroduce them to Oregon because they will eat up all the game and livestock. We discussed the old logger with a big grey beard and a metal hardhat who nearly rammed into two trucks because of exiting the wrong way after dumping his load on the MRF floor, and commented on the variety of characters we see every day. We reminisced about Paul who'd lost his excavation company after the economic collapse, and whom after he'd been hired on as a temp, used to come in drunk and operate the mini. He was the fastest, most efficient operator many of us had ever seen, but his attitude sucked and he was always drinking till 2 am every night, coming in to work at 5:30 and telling us how hungover he was *over* the radio, still sad to see him go the morning he got fired because he'd hit his 600 hours and the old felony surfaced. We talked about elk we shot, where we shot them, tags and locations, complaining how much it all cost, and cougars and bears and their tracks seen while on the hunt, and which mom and pop meat packer does the best job for the least money. I spoke up for wolves and the spotted owl, and on cue, they gave me shit for it. We talked about how expensive trophies are to mount. I'm sure there was plenty more covered I'm not remembering.

A dry spell

The water truck at 5:30 in the morning is a crippled beetle snuffling, or maybe a tortoise nosing iceberg lettuce. I operate it practically blind, moving the levers to send water to various nozzles working off memory, trusting to the dark and my instincts. The wiring harness and the PTO were ripped out after Doug ran it behind the tipper through trash and the undercarriage snagged on an old mattress, the drive line tangling everything in bared bedsprings. The mechanics did the minimum to get the truck up and running, fixing the PTO, but not the lights, complaining that that would take another day. The headlights only work intermittently, so when I drive it down the backhaul road and cut off to the road down toward the wetlands it's as if the truck sniffs its way or by feelers senses to stay on the road turning at the pumphouse station, which has a sentry light. I stop before the locked gate and get out to open it, where I see the moon and the stars and sense the ducks and the trees which surround series of interconnected ponds adjacent the Tualatin River. These trees have rookeries of great blue herons. As soon as I park the truck under the hangman's faucet and fire up the pump, I hear squawking, a bird startling awake, probably the herons, but it sounds close enough to be coming from the blackberry brush or cherry trees a few feet away which I stare at, on cue, blindly as if there were something to see. Seems like something is broken every step along the way. Even the largest pond is low and the pump struggles to pump, alternating sucking water with air, and I look up at the stars where only the brightest still shine and one is probably a planet, note the phase of the moon and struggle to make out features, then look out at the tree line and the horizon where the sun will soon come up. Somehow this sky reminds me of a show that came on at bedtime during my childhood, but I was up just long enough to see the opening credits where the cartoon of a beautiful blonde witch rides sidesaddle through an indigo sky littered with twinkling stars above an urban cityscape spelling a word with her broom. A child thinks of night like this, full of wonder, magic and innocence and longs to stay up and wander outside. And I have that feeling every morning here of nostalgia, forty years later. It has not rained for ninety days and already it's October, but a storm's coming. And every morning as I leave the pump the road faces the backside of a house bordering the landfill at the northeast corner and I have the opportunity to peer through their back sliding-glass door which allows me to watch a family eating breakfast before work or school. Two children sit before bowls while their mother is in the kitchen making lunches or stands over them talking while their dad drinks coffee or looks over the newspaper. Later that morning, wetting down the concrete pile for the grinder, the water pump fails and the truck dies dumping coolant below the engine, and won't start again because a fire erupts in the turbo. Someone discovered an eye washed up on a beach in Florida—it was the size of a softball according to reports—no one knows but speculation is that it came from some great fish, or a whale, or squid. And this makes the news.

Humming *Kokomo*

If you don't shine you are darkness.

—Charles Wright

On our way to the Army Navy beach on Ocean St.

One of the best beaches in the world eight miles away, and we're driving to it, outfitted with sunscreen, short lawn chairs,
                                    books towels and suits we are ready.
It's fun to admire the beach houses
                       —little bits of heaven—new ones going up,
some run-down, neglected needing repair. But standing
coveted real estate proud
                                   in disrepair.

Only one thing is wanted. We must stop
at Vista's CVS drugstore
                         on the way to buy my sons
                  some sunglasses to dampen the glare.

We all go in but I quickly get bored with it—come back out—
                                              to wait,
take a closer look at the car parked next to me.

In it a woman thinning greying hair, wrinkles, pale in a grubby sweatshirt and wears a mask even though the mandate is past. She fidgets like a person out of place. The old car is banged up. She gets out goes to her trunk and messes around with stuff in there. Takes something out gets back in the car, windows rolled up (she reminds me vaguely of my mother. A life without poetry).

Mine down—it's hot. I realize the situation. Sadness—
                                           nothing to do or say.
I could pray but don't because it feels so hopeless. I can't convince myself
                                    believe it might actually matter.
Since I keep thinking about it—giving it my attention—perhaps this is prayer?
I can't not watch,
                not feel it.

Furtively busy but not really doing anything, that I can tell, she's gotten out, rummaged in the trunk and gotten back in again

Then everyone comes back wearing sunglasses,
                                            laughing.

Somehow this shames me—
                              and I'd like to hush them.

We're on the way to a beach, to blue skies,
warmth, and light blinding on
                        beautiful waves rolling in over
                                            and over
the glowing shimmer of sand.

On highway 78 now my son cues up The Beach Boys and Wilson sings, *Aruba, Jamaica,
ooh I wanna take ya
Bermuda, Bahama, come on pretty mama*

Days, weeks later, I circle the landfill, catch myself humming this. . .not consciously
—numb.
                                        but I see her still, burning in the bright kiln
caged in her car radiant and wavy with heat,
                                    a fired pot whose glaze glows, an offering
furnaced and holy.

Overtime

Someone up the chain decided we should begin mining our site, the theory being for cost effectiveness to simultaneously reduce fill volume and reclaim nonferrous metals like accidentally discarded gold and even aluminum, which is far easier to find and mine from landfills brimming with tossed pop cans than to refine the ore from bauxite. Not to mention the effluvia of iron and steel—every bit of material removed leaving more space for new trash. Whole machines from demolished factory floors and pieces of used up heavy equipment lay scattered and buried throughout the site like fossilized metal mammoths. The thinking was that since we received trash during the day, we could be open for mining at night after business hours. More for less, of course. The thinking was that we could work overtime and do double shifts or split shifts alternating our weeks with day and night hours to accomplish this new policy and the gaping holes dug and mined by night could be filled in by day. It was a beautiful plan and the logic was unusually sound—more so than the usual bureaucratic bluster and inefficiency from above (actually below, since our orders came from Houston). Since our site received only C&D waste (construction and demolition) we were prime candidates for new policies and the Northwest, because of EPA regulations always turned out to be the guinea pig of forward-thinking execs. We turned out MRFing prototypes faster than Silicon Valley turned out digital technology under Moore's Law.

Once the operations began, however, things quickly unraveled—crews became confused by the blurring of day into night and night into day, heightened by the job's already tedious work and methodology. The hoary weight took a heavy toll not even huge doses of coffee, energy drinks and cigarettes or chew could assuage or overcome. Some of the crew began putting back recyclables instead of pulling them out whether out of spite or recklessness couldn't be determined. The hostility between landfill and MRF crews worsened, and when we thought morale couldn't suffer any more—it did. The holes that were excavated began to expose huge oceans of methane, far more than we could ever be expected to fill in or cope with the next day, and purple waves of it began tumultuously to rise and slosh. The sulfuric acid and dioxides from rainwet gypsum and waste drywall melted the soles of our boots and burned holes through our protective gear, ruining our lungs and our eyesight. Crews working at night had less supervision and therefore no accountability, because no one but peons were willing to work nights—those peons who refused quit or were fired. Those on duty who remained began to drink while on duty and learned to sing chanteys while they worked. The answer to the question of what you do with a drunken sailor, if raised at all, seemed obvious—give him more Bacardi. The pits dug and material being conveyered out and fed into the trommel were incredible—entire cities rested in layers below the ground, sewer systems, vaulted catacombs and crypts. Accordingly, vast numbers of corpses surfaced, floating, and even a Ferris wheel along with wings of a jumbo jet. The treasure recovered boggled the mind and I began to question if we had dug too far. We wore gas monitors whose screeching alarms never ceased, but our breathing and health seemed not to be permanently affected. We knew we had all inhaled lungfuls of asbestos and those who smoked on the job called the rest of us pussies for bringing the question of health or safety up, if we ever did. No one who thought or said anything ever spoke up because we realized no one was listening. Besides, the haul of booty was astounding and the crew pocketed anything they liked, so long as it was small enough to carry and stash into one's vehicle. There were ancient artifacts, whole coin collections, jewels, electronics, and libraries full of books extant from before the sacking and fire at Alexandria, and relics of religious and great historical significance. Masterpieces previously unknown or long forgotten were unearthed beyond our dreams' wildest imaginings. We knew by what we were finding we were not asleep on our feet. We just kept on excavating, going deeper and deeper, and some built great sailing ships using dumped phone poles for masts and fashioning black tarps used for cover for sails. After the hole reached a point where we could no longer see to the other side and daylight failed to come they launched out over the sea with grappling cranes and implements of navigation and discovery ashipboard. They threw out sounding lines that never touched bottom. It must be like sailing a great storm like the eye of Jupiter or some other gas giant. Sometimes in moments of disorientation or hallucination brought on by fatigue, we confused the ground with the night sky and sky with ground and we felt as if we floated. Bets were placed which would come first: Hell or Port-aux-Français? To me it seemed as if we were traveling back in time, because the glinting stars and constellations gradually warped and shifted shape, and the creatures swarming around us, swimming the waters of gas were larger and more primitive than the rats and skunks and gulls we commonly saw lurking on the edges of night, or even during the day—these nocturnal creatures glimpsed in the purple and indigo fog had great jaws and teeth and I could make out tentacled and segmented crustaceans that skittered quick like cockroaches just past the reach of lanternlight, some of which had an appearance like monstrous sowbugs— massive trilobites or multilegged, clawed and bony-armored fish. I wanted to capture them, and like Linnaeus, catalog and name the new species, but I was never sure if they were poisonous and didn't trust my HexArmor gloves. Secretly I was glad they feared the light, drawn but shying away.

Then one night a shout arose, "Burgess shale, boys! By God, we've struck Burgess shale!"

Charles Hood on landfills, excerpted from an email

I lived with Inuit once on St Lawrence Island, between Nome and Siberia, and they had a general dumpsite for bones going back 100s and 100s of years. Antique ivory is (was?) legally worked at least by native people, so they wanted old walrus tusks, and went back into the bone pits to find it. But nothing systematic, each random family dug up something until they got bored or hit permafrost, so there was an entire field of black wet mud gravel cratered by a hundred excavation pits, which in turn had filled up with water. And bones everywhere. Not a human cemetery, that was the other side (and had visible bones too), just thousands of ribs and shattered skull plates from seals, walruses, whales, fragments and whole ribs, sticking out of the black mud like the way artillery in WW I destroyed a trench and all the guys in it.

One pit was covered with ice, I was crossing it, and I broke through, went in up to my neck. Was wearing fleece and wool, was okay in terms of hypothermia when I got out, but I can't swim and it was just quite the shock, to be well and truly down in the bone pits like that. Cold slime and old bones, very primordial fear.

DH Lawrence has a story about a man who can't swim trying to save a drowned woman in a really foul pond in winter, same feeling.

Europa

I

Dark cracks in the bare whiteness of ice—fissured and parallel lines of paired ridges criss-crossing one another, kilometers deep, crusting over a liquid water ocean warmed by volcanic vents—these wounds which re-open and freeze closed again due to tidal movement. Some surmise strange complex life may swim these deeps under what we can see of Europa's bright scratched surface. Perhaps organisms are buried in ice scattered like trilobites in shale or the cartilage remnants of a megalodon in sediment rising to the surface, through the breaking and rebreaking ice fissure walls. Maybe the equivalent to a candy wrapper or stuffed toy, a used hypodermic or photograph like we find so many of in earthly landfills.

II

He says Shakespeare will be unread in a hundred million years. He says Europa will be the new Maui in five billion years because by then the sun, a red giant, will envelop the earth and be warming up the outer reaches of the solar system. All Europa's ice will melt making the ocean balmy on this satellite waterworld. The views of Jupiter will be spectacular, the only problem might be lack of atmosphere, but with oxygen masks, a minor detail.

Being loaded

Paying attention, which is a form of love, I think, may just be the most holy thing we can do.
— Dan Gerber

Morning headlights stare yellowed dimly—
illuminate through crusted splatters of mud.
I'll take this over halogen. Feelings matter here.

Halogen so cold, stark, less lantern or ember like,
less suited to the underworld we inhabit.
With halogen one can see, but inhuman,
more befitting a clean room or operating theater.

What he says gets sliced off hurried on either end by the keyed mic
the sound I get clipped guttural angry—a low machined growl
Usually I must check this with, *Did you just call the trailer?*

Fury the animal,
an aneurysm hiding in his chest or head,
waiting to show itself. . .lurks like a lion.

I return, my truck and I make our descent into the tunnel bowel,
lit poorly all the lights' bulbs burnt out, walls of concrete rise
up to enclose us, dark wheel-rub shadows have marked the walls,
and as we roll slowly into the water a miniature tsunami precedes me rolling away before
the truck to run up the ramp before sloshing debris backwashes in a rush—
a nuisance of rain with nowhere to go—meaninglessness—
nothing is here on purpose. Just bad engineering—
drainage lines too small so the pump seized the first winter of operation.
Management can come up with no workaround.
Brake shoes corrode, axle oil turns to milk,
brake cans suck in plastic scraps, leachate, ruining diaphragms.
Soon enough raw rainwater acidifies, blackens smells, foot and a half deep
reaching past the breaking point only then a low-level mechanic gets called in
dedicates some hours pumping it up and out onto the pad above
to drain blackening the residual pile Troy's hoe rests on; later fed into trailer.

Trailer's ready, I say.

Up there, in the firmament above dark dank concrete and water
is clamor and racket, shakers bouncing, roll-offs dumping,

and underneath all that, a hum and whine of the swingdrive,
the loader's shrill Brigade backup alarm,
a finer ta-pocketa-pocketa of residual remaining falling off the overs
end of the conveyer—all of this over my head down in the cavern
of the tunnel like some enormously long birth canal. My job description:
company colon. 53' of it. My place, rectum. Depends on the day.

Then the *whump* and jar and heave and jostle as bites of trash get dropped into
the front or belly or the tail of the possum-belly. The crash or thump and roll as
something the size of a smart car is dropped in, or sometimes a loud clatter as
metal or concrete hits and bounces on the aluminum floor, denting, punching holes,
piercing walls never patched. Nose to rear. The initial bounces reverberate throwing
me sideways, jars seat like punches to the small of the back so that I'm slapped to
attention before a lull of softer shakings. The electric hum of the swing drive which
is really diesel-powered hydraulics meaning the equipment and operator in the cab
spins above his tracks, and stick and boom shudder and wobble, jerky, loud, because
the loose pin bearings are egg-shaped rather than rods. The thumb and bucket bark
and bang open and closed metal against metal.

Diesel under electric under hydraulics, like a kind of person, or enhanced shell
around a person folded into machine. Seven minutes in I get the muffled elided call
over the two-way—incomprehensible but like an alarm or buzzer or light it signals to
me all that's necessary to know.

He is saying, *Trailer loaded,*
but the repeater translates it as a single syllable.
Keyed mic pressed in and out too quick, lazy, catching the middle like a
curse of static voicing every petty exasperation
hours of tedium
bitter anger
which says clearer than words

How the fuck did I get here?
Why do I stay?
Too good for this.
No better options.
Out of choices.
I hate my life

but would prefer not to leave it.

And I think: At home is a second wife with step kids. Just as fucked up.
Annual attempted escapes to Vegas or Punta Cana
where tourists are killed, poisoned by locals with tainted alcohol
maybe get shot by a lone gunman shooting down on a crowd at an open-air concert.

When he goes on vacation I go on a kind of vacation.

The stripped syllable abbreviated never admits any of this
but communicates a clipped pantomime says

There isn't anything anywhere better I can see
unless I win the fucking lottery.

or what I see

With this job I buy myself a new car every six months!

Whump. My formulaic well-enunciated mechanical reply: *Thanks.*

Fury can be a holiness. Furious and holy.
He doesn't know he's about to explode. Hates it
but stays, hating it. Smoldering embers
like the stub on the end of his American Spirit burning
him from the inside out and this holiness is
fury ill-expressed. I have seen this here
so many times before. This particular variety of white
star core fusion of wrath, a refined tedium and bent love
pulled out through the middle of *Trailer loaded.*

Like I don't get it.

What he means is a love so white hot
you become inarticulate with it. Bestial,
running his equipment on instinct alone.

Autopilot—we like to say.

But this is what I want to say, *Troy, bro... Don't explode!*

*We are like some deaf person hearing,
garbling the words, then guessing.
And the heat of what we feel some dark Holiness
cloaked behind this blind cloud of white.*

Whatever holiness is, I think of light. —Jude Brewer

Pumping gas

Every day feels like Groundhog Day

-Andrew Muhly

I walked in on a conversation between Ron, the head mechanic and his assistant, Debbie. Ron was talking about a buddy he worked with at the mill. The buddy's wife and he were on the verge of divorce, he says, and everything but the papers had been finalized and the end was coming up that week, when his truck slid off the road on his way into work killing him. Because the divorce hadn't been finalized, she collected his death benefit of $100,000. She and her boyfriend blew it all on stupid stuff—Christmas presents, new furniture, a huge plasma screen and other expensive toys. Debbie had already gone to the restroom without hearing the rest, or he was retelling it to me, "What do you think of that, Dave?"
"Sounds like she won the lottery—it's almost cliche."
"Yeah. If I won the lottery, I'd buy myself a new truck. Invest what was left. And if it was enough, I'd probably quit working here, get a part-time job pumping gas."
"Pumping gas!? Why would you do that?"
"Just something to stay busy. It'd be like you puttering around your business after you retired."
"You wouldn't last a month pumping gas. Not even one week. That's what I'm doing here, pumping gas."

Tim says,

I've been exposed to asbestos ever since I was a kid. In fact my lungs are coated with the stuff. There's no way for this virus (Covid-19) to get through all that armor. I have survived colon cancer and open-heart surgery. Sometimes I even long for something to take me out but it hasn't yet. So, I'm not afraid of this virus. I'm not worried about Mother Nature—I'm more worried about self-inflicted wounds.

***

I worked in the woods at fifteen, then at a mill for seventeen years, then construction in '82, finally to come to work here in 2003. If my wife were alive, I wouldn't be here either. The job gets me up in the morning, keeps me going. If she were still alive we'd be up to something around the house.

***

You may have to put on your big boy pants.

***

One saw has three handles so two can stand across from one another to straddle a great tree to bring it down together.

In those days we were cutting old growth, closer to a century ago every day. Now the sawmills aren't even fitted to mill the large logs anymore—except for the specialty outfits.

Usually doesn't pay to haul it—you'd have to haul the big stuff to Springfield. Better to log toothpicks.

Dual handle [Matella?] with a six-foot blade and you could attach a handle on the bar. Worked really well with a winch, get trees you couldn't reach otherwise.

Three man crew
connect up a 3/8" arch line and tag line
Stihl is the Cadillac of saws
the loggers like Husqvarna now
Goddamn snot-nosed kid,
I was driving logging trucks
so I must've been eighteen or nineteen
working the Tillamook burn
good work when I was younger.

***

It's kinda like one of those deals like huntin an elephant with a baseball bat.

***

Find a snowplow and follow it—cowboys gotta have their beer...

***

We didn't have power steering or AC or air ride seats in the old days. Logging trucks cooled their brakes with water. Better not run out of water.

***

After the deer are done with the apples, they move on to the pears.

Five

The world is a landfill, and in a landfill is the world

This is no longer about poetry or a prose poem; this is where my thoughts lead me as I drive around the landfill, circling like a red-tailed hawk overhead, a man-made-machine circling in a bigger machine. A metaphysical Pessoa who stashes page after page away in his infinite trunk.

***

The Air Force dumped the incinerated partial remains of at least 274 American troops in a Virginia landfill, far more than the military had acknowledged, before halting the secretive practice three years ago, records show.

The landfill dumping was concealed from families who had authorized the military to dispose of the remains in a dignified and respectful manner, Air Force officials said. There are no plans, they said, to alert those families now.

The Air Force had maintained that it could not estimate how many troops might have had their remains sent to a landfill. The practice was revealed last month by The Washington Post, which was able to document a single case of a soldier whose partial remains were sent to the King George County landfill in Virginia. The new data, for the first time, show the scope of what has become an embarrassing episode for vaunted Dover Air Base, the main port of entry for America's war dead.

—Excerpted from "Air Force dumped ashes of more troops' remains in Va. landfill than acknowledged" by Craig Whitlock and Mary Pat Flaherty, December 7, *The Washington Post*

[II]

Bulldoze the bed where we made love
bulldoze the goddamn room.
let rubble be our evidence
and wreck our home.

— **Heather McHugh,** from *Earthmoving Malediction*

Heavy tracks rolling over sawcut broken concrete
blossoms of bent rebar flowering
brick and mortar dumped—crushing it grinding it piling it
from sidewalk or chimney to the appropriated place for rubble after a war-zone,
tree to lumber to chunks to chips to sawdust,
ancient stump or old growth beams
dozed over (too big to grind)
or pinched by thumb and bucket swung up
and into ADT truckbed, or 40 yard roll-off box, the sorrowful grime—
haunted, the shy and otherworldly, shards and particles and detritus
desiccated, broken dismantled torn and rescinded,
muttering flapping crawling scattered
limping, peeled and portended, a
homeless camp clean-out
the contaminated smeared blackened smelly or
abandoned storage unit emptied of contents brought and tossed here
most often useful still,
the charred RV burned out exploded
the set aside for damnable refuse like boats taking on water
come to be buried locked away
stilled and silenced in this dark forever
hid from sight to rot and liquify until the day
all shall be revealed and the perishable
be swallowed up by the imperishable.

poetry fired in popcorn artillery bursts—

Hussy in elegant cursive
spray-painted on the railroad truck trailer bringing in junk ties—
Why?

Pantomime on workface—
truck brake sounds—cuckoo clock
or whale song

Mostly the beauty has to do with birds
sometimes wildflowers, or sky—
dozer tracks clatter in movement, back-up alarm shrill past earplugs

It's here I ceased to be a tourist—
somewhere along the line, went native—
futility daily bitchslaps us silly

The ones who insist on leaving
to better their station—smarter or cowards—
I will outlast them all!

Manifesto — They showed up, clocked in, endured the long slow burn—
whump on our metal backs—
showing up smells of holiness, of heroism

Like getting stabbed by four or eight knives at once—
punch-hit mid-air, the ground bounce, then the tear of beak—
the two become one

I plug my ears against the sound of work—on vacation I seek birdsong—
but please make it loud enough to bleed through the tinnitus, Lord—
My wife sweetly records for playback every subtle too high trill I can't catch.

Stored energy—like a box of bullets, some loose and rolling in the drawer

I am a wood chip trailer being asked to haul trash—walls thin as paper
—poked so full of holes I am torn, falling, like some war plane
shot out of the sky—one wing missing—shrapnel-riddled, pieced apart

If it ain't got that

A bucket for a fist
Teeth for fingers
A thumb opens and closes
A stick and boom
for arm and forearm
Oil for strength
Tracks for feet
Articulation and swing

The magnet truck pulls, all nail-packed, a bouncing shame of rebar—has lost all *joie de vivre*—

Skydiving with horses—
having to saddle them in the air—
I don't remember any parachutes involved

Image bearer—not motherfucker!
For, by the judgement you use,
it will be used for you.

No way to say it pretty—
these yellow foam earplugs
fucking useless

The shine of mudsheen blinds—
rare sunbreak on the road
after morning sleet and snow

Off-brand excavators—three identical
Doosan—each with a different head—
bucket and thumb, power pincher, rod-driver

Not really a circle it's more of an amoeba—
this truck route as site fills morphs and mutates—
Godzilla-sized eukaryote!

Clapping gloves
to knock the dust out—clouds—
around him a penumbra

He utters his purest prayer
standing on the top step of the cab
urinating into black tunnel leachate

The look of anger on the woman's face
thrusting that new children's stroller
into the bin

To be naked
and not know it—
We'll never be naïve like that again.

In darkness and fog the coyote,
sprinting—caught in headlights—to the end of the bridge—
ducks under the guard rail between posts

Small weak broken stupid mean things—
with the fall and winter rains
I become a mud dog again.

My, said the fly to the spider
then the spider repeats it back—
If I'd been a teacher instead of a truckdriver, I'd cuss a lot less.

After the stroke Keith Jarrett plays one-handed—I will use fewer words

We bury toxic waste over cell-liner, gas wells—Still, every spring they reappear—flowers,
    Lazuli Buntings!

We all know the Milky Way is on a collision course with Andromeda.
Here, now, in this place,
we see only broken things.

Forty thousand tips
Maybe more, certainly not less—
I have most certainly wasted my life

Every morning out of the shop office from the mechanics lips, well
before the workday begins, *Fucks, What the fucks!?* and *Motherfuckers*
come stumbling and falling—This *is* everyday life for them.

Winter is rain and mud, some snow—
Summer is triple digits, dust and wildfire smoke—
A year of endless potential!

I make the kill sign to Rocky in the tipper cockpit
Draw my hand like a knife across the throat forward and back—
Means last load no more; Means done for the day—

Landfill toys with eyes that watch

are witnesses, castoffs: discarded and reclaimed, brushed off,
mounted on the working machines by meaning-making men.

Bob's last day was Friday—Today! On the card I wrote, *Yay!!* His retirement cake is sweet, vanilla-iced, with a green trash truck in piped icing on it—When asked how it is, Robert says, *it isn't chocolate!?* But lots of rectangles have been cut out. Everyone still left has that white-smeared face sticky in bitterness no water or napkin can wipe off.

Ragsdale pulls out his flattened sandwich, smashed with the imprint of knuckles—
we don't know the specifics—
but we all know why

Clint's migraines: bananas, smell of skunk, perfume aisles in malls, sudden changes in brightness of lights going in or out of buildings, Cheerios—he may see spots with tails like sperm in vision, or tunnel vision where either the vision is narrowed, or peripheral with a black spot in the middle — bad ones involve lots of dry heave vomiting followed by lesser headaches.

Clint's dream is to move to Branson, MO and work at the Buc-ees' travel plaza—doesn't matter doing what. I understand all about this modesty, this aiming low. His daughter lives along the tornado alley of Pryor, OK, two hours away.

Dray Horse

because it is not proper to mourn a machine.

The roof of the cab well rusted over where the tortoiseshell cat most liked to lie.
                                                                                                     The hood grey
patched
with rust where the engine hot heated it up,
                                            places with bare shiny metal as if grinder had
at it
almost completely primer now
                                     otherwise.
At the doors where arms rested or hung over
                                               the white paint peeled and chipped and blew
away
and underneath grey,
a patchwork and piebald it was.
                              Relatively, considering age and types of work,
undented.

Moss, luminous, which liked the plastic window liner, and
                                              spaced like Harney County sagebrush,
a similar colored lichen grew
                     rich on the north side. Sticks and leafy debris clog the wiper well.

The grill plastic glued in places, like the door handle on the driver side,
                                                             which almost
stopped
working but never quite
                        had to replace. The license plate bent
then bent back after the lawnmower kept hitting it.
                                               Rear bumper with rusty hitch and faded
bumper stickers advertising the best businesses in Newberg
             (the 99W Drive-in and the oldest independent coffeehouse in Oregon.)
The bed clean but properly scratched—
                                  paint holding up better here than the rest.
So much hauling and work so many loads of things
                                    back and forth and favors to friends.
Starting every time
                    unless the battery failed.
                                            Towed away to be parted out
at the Pick n' Pull   where richly tattooed ladies earn their wages, and
finally to win you your afterlife.
                    Farewell.

Linked sonnets:

Absence like the sky, spread over everything—

I'm minding my p's and q's at work, vigilant, no slip ups.

By the time it gets to Thursday, Monday well past, and I say,
You know, we're going to get through this day.
And then we'll be done with it,
And then we're going to go home
And tomorrow it will be Friday.
Last summer I had my heart attacks
My shortness of breath
My crying fits
It was all wracked panic.

I tell you, My triceratops is still there
leading the way and guarding my truck

Cunningham catches me at the tunnel entry, says, *Did you hear?
Another fatality.*

*Get Home Safe Every Day—
 —summer safety slogan*

A loader operator ran over a mechanic walking across an open parking lot.
Loader quietly electric, (*needs some bicycle cards in the spokes!*). Shows me
the last shot, camera roll, seconds before he died. . .

The mechanic, 62, back turned, didn't hear,
operator's bucket raised high enough,
couldn't see.
        End of the day,
                operator didn't expect him there.

Cunningham says, *How do you not feel 70,000 pounds of equipment bearing down on you?*

And I say, Death swallows us but Death will be swallowed up by life one day.
                                          I say,
*This could happen to anyone, but really, around here,
I'm the last one you need to worry about, John*

Grief as salt. Or the missing loved one as salt,
missing equally from all places—just missing—all places

Apparently there is a significant amount of trash on the moon:

Junked flags laid over by the blast from a departing lander, cooked and burnt by unscreened ultraviolet rays, astronaut poop in white bags—900 pounds of it. Golf balls, abandoned moon rovers, lawn chairs. A three-pound sledge and a falcon feather. Your mother's face scrubbed clean out of family photos.

Not even Little Blackie

You know how in *True Grit* Mattie's been pulled out of a pit
by Rooster and LeBouef, has a broken arm and is snakebit—
Rooster is riding full gallop with her on the tough Texas gelding
Little Blackie through the night in an attempt to get her back to Fort
Smith and a doctor because she's lost consciousness and going to die?

Rooster is repeatedly described as a fat man.
Poor Little Blackie is overburdened but riding hard just because
the reins and bit and merciless rider are telling him to but then
after running down steep terrain he should have been walked riderless down
and over miles of flat, blind, plain in dark brilliant starlight he starts to falter
breathless, played out,
near collapse, but that's when Rooster pulls out his dirk knife
drives it into Little Blackies' withers (which is his back below the neck)
to get however many hundreds of yards more out of him. Of course
Blackie, terrified, obeys
not understanding why or what's at stake, he just runs
more out of urgency of fear, the command, and because he's prey
and the rider is predator and master, no longer friend or partner but driver—
then when that fails, inevitably, because Little Blackie has finite limits
a heart can't overrule or be overruled, Rooster adds salt, which buys
him a couple hundred yards more. Then the horse collapses dead,
as the book describes,
heart exploded. Rooster, an old (back then mid-forties was old) fat man
first takes Mattie on his back then finally cradled in his arms
running and stumbling like the horse to get closer
to the doctor and Mattie's salvation.

It's awkward and embarrassing to admit this
but sometimes I feel like Little Blackie, ridden by an angel
for whatever reason I can't possibly know or discern, driven blindly
into the night toward a destination and for some urgent purpose it's not possible for
        me to know. We say, above my pay grade,
or like my father, tongue-in-cheek, coming out of the post WW II era quoting Tennyson,
we say, ours is not to reason why, ours is but to do or die. Like Blackie,
a dumb prey animal—just a dumb workhorse but lacking Blackie's grit,
and grinding on.

But of course it's not like that
at all. That is a work of fiction.
This is just another aggravatingly bumpy road,
another trip up the hill,
another trailerload of trash,
and I'm dying, not out of breath,
but of tedium,
and other ordinary afflictions common to men my age.
I have a friend who confided to me the other day,
I've ended up becoming a protagonist in a Graham Greene novel—
and I'm quietly thinking to myself, well, you know those guys are all unwitting heroes—
saints, right? And I believe he is.
Well let's get this straight, I say to myself, That ain't me brother.
No grit here, nothing to see, no corpulent drunk of an angel riding my ass,
with someone's valuable life in the balance. Another friend
tells me I need to reckon with diminishment—
stop looking for meaning where none may be found.
Good advice. What this is
is not a crucifixion—this is not that—not even close.
And Little Blackie was most likely glue factory bound anyway,
but instead found a sliver of glory, not quite forgotten.

Moonlights

Perhaps he was the one who, last year at the Holešovice slaughterhouse, put a knife to my neck, shoved me into a corner, took out a slip of paper, and read me a poem celebrating the beauties of the countryside at Říčany, then apologized, saying he hadn't found any other way of getting people to listen to his verse.

—Bohumil Hrabal, from *Too Loud a Solitude*

This is how one should regard us, as servants of Christ and stewards of the mysteries of God. . . when slandered, we entreat. We have become, and are still, like the scum of the world, the refuse of all things.

—Paul, *1 Corinthians 4:1,13 (ESV)*

There are miracles in this world
but they are working-class, Wednesday morning miracles
that go mostly unnoticed by the priests.

—Michael Chitwood, from his poem "Flip" in *Living Wages*

Clint said

It's amazing how many problems you can fit into a can of Copenhagen.

A record rain pouring down

on hardhat, weatherproof hi-vis
jacket, and now he must tarp his
load, swiveling the tarper
to roll over grinder shavings and open
trailer top, head tilted against the wind
and drops, now he grabs the 8 ft
hooked rod to snag the straps and drop
them down the side. He gives each
strap one twist for wind, threads the
end through the ratchet, tightens it
down. Then dripping blue jeans
soaked climbs into and sits
in the cab, then he's off, rolling slow,
lit lights—first toward scale platform
to weigh—then off, out the gate—
to where? Washington?

The road's wet blows in rippled
sheets at our backs like a river
pushed up and little waves of
shining and stippling brown over
the black in gusts which is like
rushing armies retreats in panic but
no, much too fast—this is inhuman
more like water or more machine
like someone jerking dry a brush, or
shaking a hyssop branch soaked
with blood violently over an altar
leaving puddles and standing
liquid racing racing forward water lashes
in ribbons and curls over the wet
drop-pitted surface. My trailer and
truck shake with the force of all this
beating at my back rapid as the
strobe pattern alternating on the
sweeper truck crawling by.

The white whale is not a symbol. He is as real as you or I.

Melville thought of it as a mammoth—a land-dweller—
I think of it as a truck. I drive these seas
off-road in a whale and Jonah-like ride inside at war
with my whale; my machine wreaks havoc on body and spirit—Me
some mighty sperm whale's homunculus—O
muddy ribbed sides silver beneath,
pierced from within, not by harpoon—
O bellyful and bellyache—swimming
swoon—ever tighter circles in my dirty white cab—
and ponder just how much more Melville had it worse—

Rushing through the day to get to what matters

*Wilderness has no words. The unwritten pages
stretch out in all directions.*

— Tomas Tranströmer

A wilderness can be a moving truck,
but you never feel it until parked in a truckstop
waiting in line at the fuel desk.
See the man there interact with his wife,
or a man with his son in front of you
heading for the restroom;

yours at the home you are away from.

A wilderness is the café, sitting, staring before the unreached for phone,
others talking away at their lonely tables
before the food arrives.

A truck with a skull and cross-bones on the door
is a wilderness.
Also a landfill haul truck parked being loaded
in a tunnel in two-foot-
deep leachate
while it snows outside.

A promised land means time to go,
pulling up to the house
parallel parking
before you cross that threshold.

Sometimes children
are a wilderness once they've left
home or just before.

Practice hearing loss and lungfuls of dust
for 27 bucks an hour.
Practice circles within circles within
circles of meaningless work but
rushing through it to what matters most. This is

the exercise; this the discipline—

to go to the desert with no food and water to wait

upon the Lord.

This poem, too, could be a wilderness.

Rain Caps

after Melville once the whale is sighted

Leaving the tipper, a square-nosed Pete's
white redneck truck exhaust from twin chrome stacks
in ill-paired symmetry, wall-eyed
like mis-matched arms or legs, vapor
coughs unevenly past stuttering rain caps
that speak the engine's language
and unlike mute mitered stacks forty-fived,
those speaking too but without lips, these
cheerful little rain caps bouncing
up and down energetic babble like children
following the driver's foot which
commands the motor to move the engine,
turn the drive train to drive and truck's wheels to roll;
the motor's twin mouths, two ghost horses
in the traces, the left outpaced by the right plume
pushing the cap to flap smoky, vertically up
in a scream while the left sputters bouncing
mildly, a fluttering lesser twin, the starveling.

Invisible stacking leaves up little puffs in wisps
dragged along and up to ascend and join
the high visible clouds, hinges loose, working
those fist-sized metal discs like a drum kit
bopping to a beat flawless, drifts

a syncopated blue in some awe-bespoken
incidentally [*not*] mechanical jazz
blown disappearing old school, like Clifford

playing his last set just hours before and heading
for Chicago on the Philly turnpike that June night in '56,
hit heavy rain, Powell's wife driving so after jamming
they might catch some sleep,
but only nineteen, she wrecked and rolled the car—
and the three rose, leaving, I imagine
Brown's horn in his hand all the way to heaven.

Written on a Post-it by James, Oiler mechanic, and affixed to my bounced DVIR

Needs finished

Notes

A Logger, a Truck Driver and a Bow Hunter— Pat's verbal explanation loosely transcribed (a footnote):

1) Cows and does are just as likely to be pregnant in the Fall too, but very early in gestation but not obviously so.

2) There are ways to gut an animal in which you don't see the fetus. You don't have to open the womb when you gut it.

3) Hunting is about 150 lbs of meat in the freezer. This can mean a lot to folks who bought a tag or tags, spent money on the trip and live on tight budgets.

4) Hunting is about family and friends gathering together to share in a hunting expedition. It's family relationships, communal and tribal, kinship, and food gathering and times of fellowship and camping out with a collective aim.

5) Comprises and allows for time in the wilderness together and roughing it, and the beauty of nature and connection with it.

6) We all buy meat in the grocery store where someone else did the killing, gutting and butchering.

7) When I was young it was about competition and getting a kill. As I get older I don't care so much whether I bring home a kill or a trophy or the meat as much as enjoying the communal aspects and being out in nature feeling part of it, and the beauty.

8) Certain tags apply to buck or doe, or both, and seasons in the fall and winter are hunting with bow and then rifle respectively in order to give everyone a chance to get their animal, and ensure that if you missed an animal in the fall you can come back in winter and try again. The tags are also specific to regions. And more and more expensive.

9) Populations need thinning and deer are more prevalent in farming areas and less prevalent in forests and wilderness areas because the food and grazing are easier in farming areas and closer to people and civilization, like the Willamette Valley for example.

10) Animals are not the same as people. They do not operate on the same cognitive levels.

Pat describes an elk bugling: the poets/poems referenced by me in this poem are "Elk in the Field" by Michael McGriff, from his collection *Eternal Sentences*, and "Bull Elk in October River" by Chris Dombrowski, from his collection *Ragged Anthem*.

I sit reading: The book was *Gorgon* by Peter D. Ward

Protocluster was inspired by a *Los Angeles Times*' article reprinted in the *Oregonian* by Deborah Netburn titled, *Galaxies Head for Collision at Universe's Edge*.

I wanted to interrupt: The book was *Although of Course You End Up Becoming Yourself*, by David Lipsky. This book was also adapted into a good film called, *End of the Tour*.

Merton's teasels. I'm referencing the cover of Thomas Merton's famous book, *New Seeds of Contemplation*, in which his photo of teasels is featured on the cover.

Rejoice, O Florence, since you are so great is the opening line from canto 26 of Dante's *Inferno* (Robert Pinsky translation).

Apparently there is a significant amount of trash on the moon: was inspired by an article, from the *Oregonian* reprinted from the *Tribune News Service* by Chabeli Herrera titled, *The Moon Is a Graveyard of Apollo Astronaut Trash.*, July 18, 2019.

Linked sonnets: The title of the first and the last lines of the second reference phrasing and concepts from C.S. Lewis' *A Grief Observed*.

The white whale is not a symbol. He is as real as you or I. is excerpted from *Why Read Moby-Dick? by* Nathaniel Philbrick.

Mini Glossary

DVIR: Driver Vehicle Inspection Report

MRF: Material Recovery Facility

PPE: Personal Protective Equipment

Residual: The waste material which remains after sorting and extraction/recovery of recyclables.

Z-Wall: An elevated driveway/pad where residential customers go to dispose of mixed household goods or construction waste without a lot of pre-sorting. This separates public dumping from commercial dumping areas—the customers and their waste—and includes cardboard, electronics, motor oil, waste lumber, paper, roofing, appliances and metal, or any miscellaneous household items excluding food or food-related trash. The hope is to pull out and recover recyclables. So named because roll-off boxes (53-yard metal containers) are lined up and staggered in Z format, below a platform lined with a railing to prevent customers falling into the boxes, which means they must throw items over a 3-foot rail. The boxes are staggered so that roll-off trucks can pick up full and drop empty replacement boxes below the customer dumping area—from an aerial view would look like: Z

        Z
        Z
        Z . . ..Etc.

Acknowledgements

I'd like to specifically call out and thank the following people for invaluable help and time and effort reading through various incarnations of this manuscript and offering suggestions for improvements:

More recently, looking at chapbook manuscript drafts I received invaluable help and commentary from JR Pearson, Massimo Fantuzzi, Zeke Sanchez, Paul Nelson, Nancy Christopherson and Dan Liberthson.

Thanks to The Tipped Chair poets who regularly met with me at The Cottage Drive-thru Conference room, including Joseph Clair, Susan Easterly, Craig Goodworth, Keith Hansen, Ed Higgins, Colleen Jeffery, and Lynn Otto.

Thanks to Bernie Meyer, Gina Ochsner and Geronimo Tagatac of The Hornet Ct. group.

Thanks to the many poets posting on *Critical Poet* who offered faithful help over several years reading and commenting on earlier drafts of individual pieces, and especially Pam O'Shaughnessy.

All of you transformed poetry in my life from a lonely outsider's individual art to a communal practice of conversation, argument, and inspiration over the long haul.

Also a big thank you to Amy Casey to reproduce her artwork, for use as the cover image, *An Abundance of Caution*.

Thanks to the Pucketts at Aubade for being willing to re-up with me, and all their kindnesses.

Thanks finally to the editors and journals where the following poems appeared previously:

Triggerfish Critical Review, Issue #9: "Overtime," "Deinonychus," and "Death of bowling and the various use of heads"

The Red Wheelbarrow, #14: "Vectors" and "Dray Horse"

The Red Wheelbarrow, #15: "Pat describes an elk bugling"

Cholla Needles, #89 (May, 2024): "Ars Poetica, or, Explaining the utility of books to Pat, a non-reader," "A record rain pouring down," "Not even Little Blackie," "Apparently there is a significant amount of trash on the moon," "Holiness of landfills," "Hobo," "Not empty," "The Lazuli Bunting," "Lunchroom talk," "Bad is bent good," "Protocluster," "Selecting a reader"

About the Author

Dave Mehler studied literature at the University of California, Santa Barbara, and currently lives in Newberg, Oregon. He is the editor of the literary journal *Triggerfish Critical Review*. His chapbook *God Truck Nature* appeared in the chapbook anthology *Burning Gorgeous: Seven 21st Century Poets*, edited by Pamela O'Shaughnessy. He acted as an administrator at the popular online global forum/workshop *The Critical Poet*. More recently, he served on the board of the Oregon Poetry Association. His first full-length collection of poetry, *Roadworthy*, was published by Aubade Publishing near the end of 2020. He is presently at work on a manuscript of love sonnets called *Cloud Street*. He still works as a driver at a landfill near Portland.

www.ingramcontent.com/pod-product-compliance
Lightning Source LLC
Chambersburg PA
CBHW081449070526
44586CB00019B/2279